ism

NEO·FEUDALISM
THE CANADIAN
DILEMMA

GERARD S. VANO

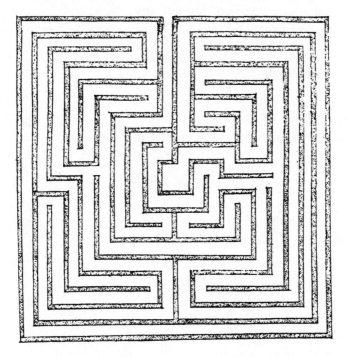

Anansi   Toronto

Cover design: Joss Maclennan
Author photograph: Robert Alsop

Published with the assistance of the Canada Council and the Ontario Arts Council, and printed in Canada for
House of Anansi Press Limited
35 Britain Street
Toronto, Ontario M5A 1R7

Canadian Cataloguing in Publication Data

Vano, Gerard S., 1943 -
  Neo-feudalism

ISBN 0-88784-088-4

1. Canada - History.   2. Ideology - History.
I. Title.

FC158.V36   971   C81-094237-2
F1024.V36

1   2   3   4   5 / 87   86   85   84   83   82   81

For my father

CONTENTS

Preface   9

Chapter One: Notes on an Ideological Crisis   11

Chapter Two: The Myth of Canadian Liberalism   21

Chapter Three: Pluralism   60

Chapter Four: Nationalism, Liberalism, and History   95

Chapter Five: (Anti-)Canadianism and
                Popular Canadianism   112

Conclusion   138

Notes   146

Selected bibliography   151

Preface

My contention is that Canada, like several other identifiable parochial societies, has never experienced the liberalization process and has never fully shared in the classical Western tradition of universal progress and human betterment through the mastery of nature. Because the conventional tendency has been to regard Canada as essentially liberal — to wear, as it were, the filtering spectacles of the liberal ideology when evaluating its history — the perception of Canadian reality has been distorted. To understand social development in this country, one must step outside generally accepted historical conventions and reevaluate our ideological assumptions, especially if we are to comprehend the current Canadian possibility of constitutional disruption and other ominous signs of breakdown and drift.

Thus only one chapter, the second, may be classed as truly "historical" in argument and citation of sources. Such an approach seemed appropriate in this instance since so much of the subsequent argument demands that we first establish Canada's early detachment from the liberal Western tradition. Like other societies outside the Western mainstream, Canada has not developed progressively in either the liberalistic or Marxist/socialist sense, but has managed instead a "side-stepping" developmental tendency, consistent with its feudal pluralism. Thus my approach in chapters other than the second departs from the more usual historical methodologies, although historical reference points are cited everywhere along the way.

This inquiry into Canada's ideology would not have been possible without the comments of numerous readers and friends over the years, with special thanks to RIK Davidson for his ongoing interest. I am also indebted to the Ontario Arts Council for its grant supporting the typing of the manuscript, to Ann Wall and the staff of House of Anansi, and to James Polk for his painstaking editorial assistance. For all errors, omissions, misrepresentations, and misinterpretations, I alone am responsible.

Gerard S. Vano
Guelph
Ontario

Chapter One:

Notes on an Ideological Crisis

I

An endless debate has plagued Canada concerning the country's association with either the European tradition or the American. The apparent choice has confounded many commentators. They have looked to different points of ideological departure for their theories, notably to the alleged evolution of a Europe liberalized and liberated from feudalism, or to the United States, once the universal society, developing from a classical liberal foundation. It is evident that in the West, England, France and the United States have been able to legitimize to some degree the philosophy of progress, or classical liberalism, and to depart successfully from the most obvious manifestations of medieval feudal society. Of course, this departure gave rise to tension between the liberalistic universal ideal and the parochial reality, but the concept of universally progressive evolution seems to be taken for granted by many historians. At least, Canada's dilemma has seldom been examined in the light of liberal progress warring with parochial feudalism. Rather, the debate has been mired in a dispute over which tradition, American or European, Canadian society replicates. It is time to re-evaluate conventional historical perspectives through a new comprehension of the complex relationships among feudalism, liberalism, and, in fact, the very concept of "history".

Certainly, parochialism, with its feudalistic foundations has been rooted in a way of life strongly characteristic of eastern and central Europe and of Canada. In these areas traditional diversity has never passed away although it has been restructured by momentous events over the past five or six centuries. The essential parochialism of the areas peripheral to Western Civilization — eastern Europe and Canada — has remained intact and, indeed, has been recently strengthening. However, the usual historical approaches to parochialism are not entirely helpful. Liberal historians assume necessary "progress", and in illiberal hands history remains largely a captive of fable, eschatology, secular theology or genuine religion. In medieval times, historical thinking was reduced to theology and chronology; later liberalization imposed a progressive *raison d'être* that, in turn, introduced a new, often unrecognized sense of limitation on history and rendered it the subordinate of progressive ideals. Still more recently, just as the contemporary West is facing a crisis of direction having lost its classical liberalistic *raison d'être*, so is its propaganda instrument, history, analogously troubled. History once preached implicitly and without question the benefits of universal liberalism for Mankind. Such is no longer so.

The marriage of the liberal ethic in the United States over the past century or thereabouts to the reality of industrial corporatism has created an infinitely dynamic social engine which has transformed the world, especially in an economic and technological sense. But what the United States has never been able to convey to others has been the indigenous liberal ideology that has set it apart from other lands. If, within the context of the West, one accepts the equation of liberalism to modernity in all senses — ideological, economic, political, constitutional, social, and cultural — then the United States has been the only truly modern country. Its liberal modernity has been closely associated since its founding with the metaphysical notion of social and ideological universality and with the mastery of nature for the benefit of humankind. It has been argued — as it will be here with qualification — that the United States has been a nation state: this is a partial truth which merits appropriate refinement relative to the concept of universality.

By its very nature, classical liberalism has been an ideology with universal overtones: it has been the veritable antithesis of parochialism, of limiting ethnicity and racism, of stultifying class concepts, of constraining localism and provincialism. The United States does consist of fifty politically and geographically limited states each of which is, so to speak, potentially an autonomous national unit, but the United States has been inclined toward *functional* universalism for most of its existence in its expansive notions of Manifest Destiny, in its willingness to accept foreigners on a fraternal, egalitarian basis, and in its according of full stateship as opposed to colonial status to political units associating with the Republic. Although the United States has been reduced to genuine nationality in the last decade partly by reason of the limitations imposed by military failures in East Asia, until very recently with the additions of Alaska and Hawaii as states, America was more universal than national.

George Grant has critically examined the universal aspects of American liberalism and modernity with special reference to English Canada.[1] Grant too hastily has assumed the necessary demise of conservative or traditional societies in the progressive age. According to Grant, the liberal quest for individual liberation from environmental "fate" or "chance" — and into whose service technology has been drafted — has created a closed system in which the very pursuit and promotion of that technology has become an end in itself. Instead of the liberation of Mankind envisioned by early liberals, the "liberating" technology of America has imposed its own distinct type of tyranny, the tyranny of a monolithic ideology with correspondingly limited judgments and perspectives which brook no fundamental criticism. Nor does that ideology permit the entertainment of any doubt concerning material betterment and technological progress. So integral has the drive to progress become, together with its foundation, the creation of new technologies, that it has virtually become a public religion.

Nor, according to Grant, have the *conventional* left and right (ie socialism/Marxism and liberalism, respectively) differed fundamentally in according supreme reverence for mitigating the ills of the human condition through continuing technological advance. Like the liberal modernizers, Grant does not entirely divorce, in his own conceptual system, liberals and Marxists who both believe in progressive materialistic betterment; as Grant indicates, Marxists and liberals provide no genuine alternatives, even if they do happen to disagree on superficialities such as the existing social and economic arrangements. What has been lost by modern man in his technological system with its necessary devotion to progress has been the ability to subscribe to a differing value system or to question the imperatives of the technological system, itself. For Grant, liberal America with its commitment to human liberation on a universal scale together with its techno-logical capacity, had necessarily (and paradoxically?) become, in its own right, an imperial power. But Grant wrote against the background of the war in Vietnam which influenced his judgment. Time — really a very short time — has raised questions about the assumed and necessary march of (liberal) modernity.

There has been an ingrained tendency or preoccupation in historical study to structure circumstances around a notion which has been at once progressive and universal. In this regard, the very sense of history — or rather a liberal sense of history, since one is *de facto* indistinguishable from the other — has imposed a limitation on the historical perspective, itself. Grant noted the paradox of America questing for emancipation as it imposed a new tyranny of judgmental deprivation based on technological imperatives. One could well broaden that deprivation to include historical study, which has repeatedly assumed the existence of, and imposed a sense of, progress. In truly historical societies, this tendency has merely coincided with discernable reality. All societies, however, have not been truly historical because all societies have not been *ideologically* progressive. The liberal and/or modernistic vision of the global communities moving "forward" into a singular, progressive, and emancipated social condition is simply not happening. Historical study with its ingrained sense of progress has dictated the existence of history where it has not been an actual or functional condition of the prevalent socio-ideology. While empirically verifiable change has undeniably influenced every global society through the example of, and interaction with, the

West, surely it is valid to question the widely held but unthinking equation of change to progress and/or modernization. This assumption has characterized a vast body of literature which has evolved under liberal and Marxist influence whose foundational concepts are based on materialistic flux in uni-directional evolution. This inquiry will not examine the question of progress in a global context, but will, rather, restrict itself to Western Civilization and to Canada, both of which, too often, have been improperly assumed to be modern and liberal.

II

Canadians have not generally been able to apprehend the nature of their impending modernity crisis because they have attempted to perceive and expound the history of Canada in terms of the rhetoric of Anglo-American liberalism. The latter, an alien ideology imported into Canada, has distorted the perception of the nature of Canada. The rhetorically liberal tendency has been to place Canada in the mainstream of the Western tradition and its association with progressivist notions of history has blinded Canadians and their historians to the sheer limitations of historical inquiry in assessing the socio-ideological circumstance of Canada. (The term "socio-ideology" may best distinguish ideologies arising from reality or actual circumstance, as opposed to such functional ideologies as classical liberalism, or theoretical ones such as Marxism.) It is only at present, against the background of a declining liberalism in the West, that the handmaiden of liberalism, history, has relaxed its hold and the "screen" through which Canadians have peered has been partly obviated.

The decline of Western liberalism has revealed an infinitely complex social universe, albeit one much more parochial and less congenial than that in which the classical liberals dwelt and delivered their tireless tirades against the afterglow of medieval feudalism. What contemporary liberals seem unable to perceive is the feudal revival taking place in their very midst. Since historical study has been associated with classical liberalism in its denial of medieval feudalism, one might seek the questions and answers not by merely *using* history as a method of epistemological inquiry, but by examining its conceptual relationship to liberalism. The scope of liberal history, the perspective of liberal history, the assumptions of liberal history have all, so to speak, been vital to the conventional view of Canada; as circumstance alters classical liberalism and by logical extension redefines the very epistemological concept of history, circumstance also necessarily reveals an unconventional relationship of Canada *vis-à-vis* Western Civilization, *vis-à-vis* the Anglo-American world, *vis-a-vis* the associated notions of liberalism and history.

The assumption of Canadian evolution within the context of Western Civilization has not been warranted; that assumption has not been adequate to permit a sufficiently critical evaluation of Canadian development. This difficulty has arisen because the generally accepted liberalization process in the West may not be applicable to Canada where historians have attempted to expound a comparable process which they allege started with the residual feudalism of New France that eventually gave way to British style liberalism in the form of responsible government and political autonomy. Unlike Western Europe, the United States, and Great Britain which enjoyed a measure of liberalism, Canadian history evolved, it is here contended, within an essentially *illiberal* context. This obviously precludes any assumptions about Canadian history having evolved in a fashion comparable to that of the liberal West.

For reasons to be developed in due course, classical liberalism is considered to be the left and pluralism the illiberal right; liberalism will be defined in Chapter Two, pluralism in Chapter Three. For convenience, it may be stated here that there has been a tendency to regard liberalism as pluralistic and, admittedly, there is a measure of truth in this view. But pluralism is a relative concept. If one examines the United States, its original liberal values have been more or less monolithic. More recently, the United States has become less monolithic and more complex because of industrialization. If one moves outside the context of the United States and looks across the whole spectrum of historical and socio-ideological development in the West from medieval times, one also finds in feudal illiberalism a pronounced pluralism, a society fragmented by various complex overlapping parochial values, each commanding its own group of adherents. The left represents an increasing liberal monolithism and the right an increasing pluralism.

The recent eclipse of monolithic liberalism in the United States has opened a curious possibility for Canada. New France-Canada had emerged as the virtual antithesis of The Thirteen Colonies–United States. Definitionally the two societies were almost exactly opposite; Canada was, both by indigenous choice and by British Imperial preference, what its southern neighbour was not. At its socio-ideological point of departure from 1776 to 1787 and, henceforth, well into the nineteenth century, the United States constituted the universal society. Successively, throughout a corresponding period, Canada reaffirmed its contrary parochial and illiberal qualities. But, more recently, American liberal universality has been failing and with it has come a relaxation of the countervailing Canadian antithesis. For Canada, liberalism is no longer the anathema that once it was.

Corporate-liberalism conceptually distinguishes between classical liberalism with its atomistic individualism on one hand and, on the other, both medieval feudalism with its limited social corporations and the infinite complexity of contemporary corporate industrial society. The sheer simplicity of classical liberalism has been fading as contemporary society has been assuming a rigidity and inflexibility not unlike that of medieval times. The industrial corporate quality of contemporary times and the social corporations of medieval times have certainly not been exactly similar, but both have borne a closer socio-ideological relationship to each other than has either to classical liberalism. There has been a tendency to misjudge the current regression from classical liberalism and to regard twentieth century liberalism as "advanced" or more evolved. This simply is not so; hence the utilization of terminology to stress the corporate similarity between "advanced" liberalism or corporate-liberalism and the corporate aspect of feudalism. Both corporate types have been exclusive of classical liberalism and may be considered rightward or pluralistic.

III

One dimension to the presently evolving crisis of the old order in Canada involves conflicts between various highly exclusive interests within the context of the right. Associated with this rightward instability and animosity has been a rising sense of pronounced ethnicity, class distinction, rampant provincialism and/or regionalism, in short, a form of almost medieval socio-ideological pluralism. This is not to say, however, that liberalism is not playing a role in the presently developing Canadian crisis for it is. But liberalism as a viable ideology in Canada is of very recent origin and has borne almost no relationship to the Canadian Liberal Party. Only in this century has the liberalistic process entered Canada successfully, all previous intrusions having been rejected. The arrival of liberalism in Canada has added a crucial dimension to the developing crisis. Elsewhere — in the United States, Great Britain, western Europe — liberalism has been at the very root of the best offered by Western Civilization, its institutionalized respect for individualism, its political democracy, its economic entrepreneurialism, its technological innovation. In Canada no indigenous ideological respect for the components of liberalism has been popularly ingrained because the derivative benefits of a truly liberal system were obtained in Canada relatively easily by a process of osmosis from the Anglo-American world. Largely because of these derivative benefits which were originally worked out in alien circumstances and imported already mature into Canada, Canada was largely able to forego the massive dislocations of Western society which accompanied acceptance of the liberal ideology elsewhere. However, the renewed liberal intrusion into Canada in this century is being accompanied by the general uncertainty that attended its original and indigenous arrival elsewhere throughout the West.

There is sometimes a tendency to view Canada or some of its constituent parts as derivative or replica societies. Social replication does not, of course, refer to a total objective similarity between a metropole and its colony. That would be quite impossible because local conditions are bound to dictate certain distinguishing features. Nonetheless, when the metropole and the colony experience an evolutionary tendency which has been *ideologically* parallel, a case of value transmission from the metropole to the colony may be considered to have occurred. The prime example of liberal transmission and replication has been that of England-Great Britain to the Thirteen Colonies-United States. Canada had also experienced value transmission at its inception but from a quite different non-liberal source. Since France was liberalized only after its colony was lost, the formative ideological influence in New France had been the metropole's residual feudalism. New France and its Canadian successor have consequently tended toward internal divisiveness, the ultimate results of which are just now coming into focus for Canadian society seems to be moving toward an impasse which may, in general terms, be regarded as parallel to — or even an outright replication of — that of pre-revolutionary France. The debate concerning the future of the latter had been initially carried out in the 1780s largely within the context of the right which had been growing deceptively stronger. The second estate had been attempting to bully the government into restoring that estate's feudalistic autonomy and to force the other estates to accept this powerplay. The second estate, in so doing, had equated its special interests to those of the nation. But locked into the third estate and more or less ignored was the middle class which had long been inspired by the liberalizing English and American Revolutions. In contemporary Canada as in pre-revolutionary France, what seems to have been unnoticed has been the liberalization process which, with specific reference to Canada, has come in the guise of Americanization. The major difficulty involves the fact that no orderly mechanism exists to legitimize liberalism (ie to recognize its popular support by conferring legal-constitutional substance) in twentieth century Canada. And that, of course, was precisely the problem facing France on the eve of the Revolution when all eyes were focused, unwisely, in the wrong direction.

IV

The following analysis has several conceptual dimensions. First is the overall question concerning the validity of the conventional framework for the study of ideology and history as an adequate conceptualizing and epistemological tool in its own right. It is not contended that the conventional left-right structure is totally inapplicable but that it must be rethought in light of the ideological *regression* throughout Western Civilization during the past century and for which the necessary progression from right to left in the liberal/Marxist system makes no provision.

Directly associated with the foregoing is the notion of objective historical detachment. Of course, historians have attempted "detachment" for a long time, but generally they have not come to grips with the interconnections among socio-ideology, a sense of history, and the concept of necessary progress. The idea that history is definitionally non-Platonic, if one may specifically borrow from Collingwood notions of history broadly accepted,[2] deserves closer evaluation as does its logical corollary that history is the study of change. The traditionally associated notions of change, progress, and history as uni-directional evolution must be scrutinized. That the mechanism by which this proposed re-evaluation is executed should be largely ontological ought not cause distress for it will be based on a socio-ideological model (for want of a more appropriate term) of Western Civilization.

Much of the immediately following analysis will focus on the relationship between Canada and classical liberalism. This naturally involves an examination of two dimensions of the old order in Canada. On the one hand there has been the traditional fragmenting struggle among the constituent interests of the residual feudalistic old order. On the other hand is the "late arriving" integrating power of liberalism emanating from the United States. These circumstances have generally not been recognized because the conventional perspective, conditioned by wearing the distorting spectacles of liberalism or Marxism — the modernizing and materialistic ideologies — has tended to regard Canada as an advanced, mostly Anglo-American society in the liberal Western mainstream. This assumption may be best examined by critical reference to the degree to which Canadian development paralleled that of liberalism elsewhere.

Chapter Two:

The Myth of Canadian Liberalism

I

A popular myth claims that Canada has been a liberal land. This liberalism, it has been alleged, was part of a much grander process which engulfed the Western world after the demise of the feudal period and which reached its apex in the nineteenth century. Two distinct historical schools of thought in Canada have accepted the validity of this alleged liberalization process. One school has perceived Canada as a liberalistic replica in the British tradition; the other school has seen Canada as a North American ideological associate of the United States. The pro-British school may be defined as the conservative-liberal school because British liberalism and its alleged Canadian replica never quite matured to the degree American liberalism did, and, instead, retained various pre-liberal tendencies from the feudal period, such as the monarchy and a certain respect for elitism. The pro-(North) American school may be defined as the liberal school by virtue of its stress on the similarity of common North American influences. The liberal school has, of course, recognized a measure of distinction between the American and Canadian achievements by paying proper attention to the different methods and rates of emancipation of Canada and the United States from British imperial control.

Although liberalism, it must be admitted, did differ in degree, in application, and in acceptance in western Europe, Great Britain, and the United States, several common features have been indicative of its presence. At its most elementary and universally recognized level, liberalism has been associated with atomistic individualism and, more rhetorically, with "freedom" and "liberty", whose functional social translation has permitted enormous mobility, both geographic and vertical, based on merit. Also, liberal societies have exhibited a strong predisposition towards, and respect for, individualized economic well-being. With this individualistic economic imperative has come (in comparison to the feudal ethos which preceded it) an inordinate respect for monetary power, the free market system, and the sanctity of private property. These concerns found their way into the articulation, by John Locke, of a new theory of the state in the late seventeenth century. Locke expounded the revolutionary notion that government was instituted by rational men (who were equated to those with private property) to legislate their self-seeking political and economic interests. Such a perception saw society and all its aspects — constitutional, economic, political, ideological — as being logically consistent, since all aspects were derived from a singular propertied interest.

Because of this logically integrated system of individualistic values operating both through the economic and political systems, over a period of centuries liberalization was popularly accepted and ingrained, thereby eliminating the vestiges of feudal exclusivity which had defined society not in terms of individuals but in terms of limited interest groups. As a consequence, in liberal societies (liberal in theory if not in fact), the concerns and needs of "the people" have been paramount. It has been this popular dimension which provided the basic quality in building the British and American nations, at least until the nineteenth century. In the Anglo-American world, in brief, liberalism has been, de facto, the basis of nationalism and the lengthy anti-feudal liberalizing process was a significant factor in promoting the localistic (ie nationalistic) resistance of medieval England against extraterritorial Roman Catholic imperialism and, later, of the Thirteen Colonies-United States against extraterritorial British imperialism. Associated to some degree with the struggle for national existence has been the characterization of liberal society by an indigenous leadership arising from ostensibly popular foundations and an institutionalization process whereby that leadership has learned to transfer power in an orderly fashion. Very broadly, liberalism has contained a potentially revolutionary element which has made it a respecter of innovation in technology and science and of entrepreneurialism in economics and business. If innovation and entrepreneurialism have been basic to an ideology and philosophy of modernity, then surely modernity has been rooted, for the most part, in liberalism.

That Canada has absorbed the attractive rhetoric of liberalism is not in dispute. What is in dispute is the translation — the *functional* translation — which liberalism received upon its arrival in Canada. Because historical examination has been conditioned by liberal concepts of history, progress, and necessary Westernization, most commentators have neglected to entertain the possibility that in its specific political, constitutional, military-strategic, and economic context, Canada could have followed an ideological path contrary to the west European and the Anglo-American. No inquiry which stresses (liberalistic) empirical objectivity in assessing Canadian development could possibly realize that Canada was moving away from the Anglo-American experience, because during the last two centuries Canada absorbed, by a process of osmosis, the most superficial (ie empirically evident) aspects of the liberal process — political democracy, advanced technology, and generally higher living standards — without ever, itself, liberalizing in any fundamental fashion. Nor did incentive to liberalize Canada exist: why bother with the enormous discomfort of socio-ideological readjustment like that which elsewhere attended the triumph of liberalism? Why bother, when the superficial benefits could be so readily possessed without comparable sacrifice — without civil and revolutionary wars, without those acts of public violence so absolutely essential to the fusion of diverse, often contradictory values into a single, logically consistent, liberal value system? But in foregoing the liberal agony another price has been paid. Canadian society, in a fashion vaguely reminiscent of feudal society, has remained far more vulnerable to internal disunity and extraterritorial empathy.

II

The conservative-liberal school of Canadian history had its origin in the work of Harold Innis. Almost half a century ago, Innis pointed out in *The Fur Trade in Canada*,[1] that the major economic activities were organized by Europeans, both French and English, and that this situation substantially conditioned all other social developments. The application of European technologies destroyed the indigenous social structures and made the native populations dependent on European goods in an accelerating fashion. The natives in pursuing furs had lost their own technological skill and transmitted that of the white man ever farther into the continental interior. Innis' line of thought established the staples theory of Canadian economic development; the Canadian economy, it was claimed, depended on basic commodities for export during various historical periods and received in exchange the benefits of more advanced technologies.

In terms of politics, the Innis thesis established that the institutions arising in Canada were dictated by the extractive mechanisms and by the necessity of colonial importation and distribution of manufactures. The institutions were, consequently, paternalistic and centralized. In the French period, the government, church, and seigneurial system reflected this situation. Nor did the Conquest alter the prevailing tradition, British merchants after 1760 much influencing self-seeking legislation to dominate the extractive staples economy and to reorganize the continental interior. Later, lumber and wheat fit the same pattern of a staples economy, with the government functioning to set up effective transportation systems in the form of canals and railroads which tapped the resources of the continental interior for the benefit of extraterritorial interests. Even the eventual Canadian Confederation was regarded as the result of two factors associated with the trade in staples: the tendency of mercantile interests to centralize authority for exploiting natural resources and of modern industrialism for creating the transportation and communications technologies to make possible a centralized transcontinental Dominion.

Also utilizing the staples concept was Donald Creighton[2] who has seen the connection with Britain as the necessary foundation of the Canadian nationality. In Creighton's *schema* the single greatest threat to Canada's existence has been the United States, to which Britain has acted as the counterweight. Personalities like Conservative Prime Minister Sir John A Macdonald who upheld the British connection have enormous prestige in the Creightonian system, whereas those like later Liberal Prime Minister Mackenzie King, who regarded that connection as a colonial vestige and worked to terminate it, are held in contempt. Those of King's ilk, it has been asserted, have opened the way to overwhelming American influences by upsetting the necessary counterweight. The American threat has especially manifested itself in the realms of economics, culture, and military continentalism. And, we have been assured, continentalism in any form represents the antithesis of Canada's true interest. But a position such as Creighton's, as will be eventually argued, if valid in the realm of politics and economics, is not correct insofar as it relates to ideology.

After the Conquest, the British entered Canada and adapted the seigneurial system to the staples trade based on fur. Creighton speaks of an "Empire of the St Lawrence" in which the commercial English speaking interests won out over their French speaking agrarian rivals and imposed their particular ethos, a mercantile ethos, through the institutions of the state. The predominance of staples-extracting interests is a persistent theme of Creightonian writing in interpreting Canadian history until the Great Depression. The post-Confederation National Policy was designed to facilitate the export of staples. Under Prime Minister Macdonald only that aspect of the National Policy dealing with immigration failed; but the transcontinental rail system was completed and the protective tariff erected, both being essential to the eventual wheat boom when conditions bettered throughout the world. Macdonald's dream was vindicated: he had erected a political unit in British America based on the European economy which helped Confederation Canada survive the threat of American annexation.

That situation, according to Creighton, ended in the decade after The First World War. The east-west trade axis based on the last great staple, wheat, failed, and new income sources based on minerals moving south to American factories developed. This type of enterprise, moreover, mainly aided provincial treasuries, not the federal one. The old staple-based European-Canadian economy was undermined and, so Creighton claims, with it was questioned the very existence of Canada. Once again, the economics and politics of this position may be quite valid but Creighton fails to probe deeply enough into the ideology relating to a possible collapse. Nor is this distinction of ideology as opposed to economics and politics a minor one in its Canadian context for, unlike the ideology of the Anglo-American world, Canadian ideology was not an extension of economics, and therefore merits considerable attention in its own right. Indeed, an ideological emphasis tends to indicate that Canadian problems have been basically internal and only incidentally extraterritorial.

One cannot read Creighton's writings without coming to the firm conclusion that he regards the Canadian ideology — insofar as he could be induced to reduce his perspective to ideology — as fundamentally but conservatively liberal. The unfortunate tendency of those like Creighton in the conservative-liberal school to regard Canada as "British" extends beyond a mere constitutional connection. This has caused substantial and unnecessary confusion. Because of the staples-induced constitutional and economic connections, the tendency has been to assume an ideological "Britishness" (ie conservative liberalism) which simply does not stand up under ideological scrutiny. However, Canadian society has never been liberalized, even in a conservative, "British" sense. The struggles between mercantile interests and agrarian ones which Creighton saw resulting in mercantile victories (and, he would claim, liberalistic victories) have been badly misread. If one takes the British and the Americans as examples of historically successful liberalism, then the process by which it was inculcated elsewhere was never reproduced in Canada. Nor may an ideology be passed along by a mere process of osmosis; it must be experienced and translated into indigenous institutions.

Staples-based theses are weakest in the ideological area. Did being on the receiving end of European capitalism ingrain the same ideology in the Canadian colonial as in the European capitalist? Or, to restate the dilemma: did the staples system transmit liberal values from Great Britain to Canada? And even if certain individuals active in the system were thus liberalized, did sufficient social machinery exist to transmit those values to Canadian society at large? Was the staples system even capable of producing the social machinery to popularize liberal values? It is contended here that while capitalism and liberalism may be natural allies, the mere existence of the former does not necessarily produce the latter. Indeed, those on the receiving end of the capitalistic system (ie importing manufactures into Canada) were bound to develop a quite different ideological perspective from those on the producing end. Capitalistic operations in Canada were extremely exclusive and could not, as will be shown, erect popular institutions capable of ingraining, by their very nature, a liberal ideology.

For staples theorists, the major liberalizing instrument of Canadian society has been the merchant class. This Creighton took to be the most assertive of all Canadian social classes. Shortly after its arrival in 1760, the British-American merchants, according to Creighton, set about to accomplish two objectives: to restore the St Lawrence commercial system and to obtain control of the government. But of more significance to the question of ideology is the problem of the relationship of that class to the populace. One must admit that the merchants who arrived in Quebec after the Conquest were probably as liberal as their time and historical circumstance permitted. But one must also wonder if the very staples mechanisms with which the merchants worked permitted them, aside from enhancing their liberalism, even to retain what they had. One might raise the same questions about the merchants, specifically, that one asks about Canadian society, generally: did the economic system — indeed, could that system given its exclusive staples foundation — have acted as a genuine agent of *functional* liberalism? Creighton seems to believe that an immigrant class — in this case, mercantile and Anglo-American and well on the road to liberalization — could have entered the relatively hostile environment of post-Conquest Quebec and have imposed its ideological will in addition to its political pre-dominance despite the ingrained attitudes of the long established population. Is there not an alternative and more plausible possi-bility? Could not the two — the long established populace and the arriving mercantile class — each have retained their mutually exclusive ideologies at the rhetorical level, neither really threatening the other and yet each utilizing the political and constitutional instruments in a fashion which each believed consistent with its own ideology while the other remained more or less ignorant of what actually was occurring?

Ideologies tend to filter one's view of the world. Translated into the Creightonian system this means that the merchants (and their progeny) believed that they and Canadian society, after a long struggle from 1760 to 1867 and beyond, had not only remained British but had also bestowed liberal (in the British as opposed to the American sense) benefits to the entire society, largely through economic and political-constitutional mecha-nisms. What never seems to have occurred to the merchants, or to Creighton, their historian, is that functional circumstance de-anglicized and consequently illiberalized them and Canadian society.

Confusion exists concerning the role of the merchant class and the staples trade in defining a liberal Canada because, at an earlier time, the mercantile interests in England had helped to define English liberalism. Did the Canadian mercantile function parallel the English? To have been liberal and British — best expressed by the slogan "the rights of Englishmen" — had involved meshing the two concepts into a unity where distinctions were largely non-existent because the popularizing economy of England-Britain had, from the thirteenth to the nineteenth century, dictated the integration of ideology and social reality. So too did indigenous interests in the United States popularly define their society while the comparable Canadian interest was exclu-sive and never defined a unifying integrating ideology in Canada. The central failure of staples theorists has been to assume that the mere presence of a business class is indicative of a measure of liberalization. Such has not been so.

J M S Careless, in a reply to the liberalistic frontier thesis, so prevalent a theme in interpreting American history, has expanded upon the staples theme to produce a more metropolitan approach to Canadian history.[3] While the frontier thesis stressed western influences upon the east, Careless reversed the emphasis, stressing the eastern impact in the Canadian west. Not the American frontiersman, but rather the businessman and merchant were the active agents of Canadian expansion. While it must be conceded that the city — specifically Montreal in the traditional staples context — had organized communications, trade, and finance in the continental interior, one must also ask if, in light of the adverse Canadian response to monetary capitalism, possibly the metropolitan view is not too casual? One may readily admit the ideological dimension at which Careless hints when he points to the concentration of metropolitan influences as being essential to Canadian conservatism in opposition to the "forest democracy" of the United States. But surely one must question rather critically the degree to which, and the mechanisms by which, the city influenced individuals, although it obviously "gathered in" the hinterland in which they dwelt. In Europe it is clear that the mechanisms included a merchant class, monetary power, and the capitalistic utilization of agricultural land which drew both urban and rural life into a more singular and integrated value system than had existed under feudal diversity. Arising within a long-established agrarian populace, the city became a new focal point of life, first in commerce and distribution, and later in production. If the mercantile interests represented the rising force in late feudal Europe, then the question which follows naturally involves the degree to which Canadian development paralleled that of Europe.

In a later essay, Careless claims that the old seigneurial and fur trading interests were successfully integrated into the metropolitan system based on London and that the problems which resulted in the abortive Rebellion of 1837 arose from the new lay elite which found itself excluded from substantial economic and political power.[4] The metropolitan system operating through Montreal was curiously unable to ingrain its values in the populace of the immediate hinterland. Given this evident shortcoming, one must surely question its vitality in more remote western areas. The ability of a metropolis to accomplish specific objectives in its hinterland, especially of an economic nature and involving such things as construction of transportation and communications system, is not in doubt. As Careless indicated, the influence of the city in the form of the railway preceded the colonization of western Canada. But, one might state by way of reply, this penetration of the uninhabited west, unlike the rise of cities in populated Europe, represented a "dispersal" rather than a "focalization" of effort with no consequential ideological integration. It seems evident that the traditional mechanisms of urban vitality which elsewhere made the hinterland an extension of the metropolis did not function especially well in Canada. Not until after the Union of 1840 was there any genuine effort to provide for municipal institutions. In Upper Canada, Toronto had not been incorporated until 1834 and did not assume metropolitan prominence until the 1880s. Urban vitality arrived relatively late. It is still restricted to a handful of centres and has, consequently, not really paralleled the popular urban dynamism of western Europe and the United States. The integrating characteristics of monetary capital and urbanization, it will be contended here, have been less pronounced in Canada than elsewhere.

Another metropolitan thesis with even broader scope has been expounded by A R M Lower. According to Lower, the metropolis had required a concentration of economic power which depended on colonial supplies to sustain its position of predominance.[5] According to the theory of empire arising from metropolitan predominance, a self-contained economy was to be set up, a factor which Lower believes accorded closely with the actual relationship between Britain and the remaining British American colonies after the American Revolution. This view contains the assumption of direct value transference from the metropolis to the colony; thus, if the same fundamental economy and legislation were functioning within a singular isolated system, then the colonial hinterland had surely to replicate the metropolis. This is not to say, of course, that economic results of the interaction did not differ between the metropolis and its colonies, for they did: as Lower concluded in his study of the timber and lumbering trade, Canadian forests engendered prosperity for the British timber importer and the American lumberman, who left Canada with its forests destroyed and no comparable prosperity. The staples trade — in forest products, at least — was an exploitative act which favoured the metropolis, not the colonial hinterland. But, the exploitative aspect notwithstanding, the concept of socio-ideological replication has necessarily rested on the notion of direct value transmission from the metropolis to the hinterland.

This concept of value transmission, especially as it relates to the trade in Canadian staples, constitutes a curious view of history because it assumes that all historical direction, at least in the context of what is referred to as Western Civilization, is more or less integrated, unified and singular. Lower has perceived liberalism to be an honourable concept which, in democratic societies, supplies the notions of justice and right to counter the potential excesses of democracy based on numerical superiority.[6] Tracing the historical roots of liberalism from Christianity through the mainstream of Western Civilization, Lower regards Canada as a direct recipient of this extraterritorial tradition. Lower does, of course, make allowances for minor local liberalizing gestures such as the achievement of responsible government;[7] but he sees this as a replay of the British achievement.

In this general line of historical thought, of which Lower's perception is but one example, the lands associated with the west European tradition necessarily and to some degree absorbed its evolving liberal value system. Such a perspective, however, fails to discern the possibility of Canadian society developing outside the Western ideological mainstream. In Canada the staples trade accommodated the socio-ideological situation which had long been declining in Europe. Canada provided a new lease on life for elitism, an internally divided society, and the general exclusivity of social classes so characteristic of feudal society. Given the general drift of west European socio-ideological development during the period of the trans-Atlantic trade in staples, one must try to ascertain why, in Canada, the system, within the nature of its organization, did not maintain the popularizing mechanisms to effect Canadian liberalization. For Canada to have accorded with Innis' and/or Lower's view as a product of Europe and/or (post-revolutionary) Great Britain, two features would have to characterize the Canadian ideology: it would have to be, to a substantial degree, a popular extension of economics, and it would have to exhibit an evolutionary feature toward integration and homogeneity. That does not appear to have occurred.

As early as 1774, the Quebec Act shifted British America away from integration. While Creighton did admit that the Quebec Act perpetuated an anti-commercial oligarchy, he has tended to stress the Act's more positive mercantile aspects, its provision for expansion, for example, into the Ohio valley. But one must be very cautious about using expansion as an example of a qualified mercantile victory. The real measure of success by the commercial interests was not so much the expansion of the geographical scope of commercial operations, but was related rather, in an ideological sense, to the successful establishment of an integrating social system. In that regard the Quebec Act constituted, *de facto* and *de jure*, the definitive surrender by the Imperial state itself of any pretence to inculcation of the liberal philosophy in Quebec and its Canadian successor. The colony's ideological inertia, from a functional as opposed to a rhetorical point of view, seemed increasingly thereafter less to replicate post-revolutionary Great Britain than pre-revolutionary France.

III

Commerce had played the major role in the initial liberalization of Europe and much has been said of its impact in Canada. Replying to those who have regarded the fur trade as detrimental to New France by drawing off manpower and encouraging hostility with the British colonies, E R Adair argues that the trade was the "life blood" of the colony.[8] The fur trade did not undermine industry because the colonials had no industrial interests; it did draw manpower from agriculture, but then only, Adair qualifies, those who were adventurers. Defeat came ultimately, not from fur-trading rivalry but because the British government was dedicated to worsting France. Adair also rejects Innis' view of the development of the state structure, claiming that paternalism and colonial governmental organization were not results of the fur trade but dated from the origins of the colony and were regular techniques of government. The former position is the logical consequence of

Adair's contention that the scope of monopoly has been over-stated, applying as it did only to beaver which left the rest of the fur trade in the area of free enterprise. Sigmund Diamond has contended that, after 1663, the state tried to create a planned, highly structured society. This project failed, in Diamond's view, because concessions had to be made to attract and hold a *voluntary* labour force.[9] J F Bosher has argued the revisionist thesis that confusion over the limits of the private and public domains may have subjected the state to intrusions from private enterprise.[10] The foregoing indicates the difficulty in identifying the impact of commerce and business on the role of the state and on society at large in New France.

The central question in this controversy may be reduced to more sociological terms of reference: did a dynamic Canadian bourgeoisie exist as a class and, more importantly, if it did, to what degree were its values transmitted to the rest of the colony? On one hand are Michael Brunet and Guy Fregault who assert that such a class did exist while Jean Hamelin and Fernand Ouellet deny it. Hamelin claims that colonial economic activity was a record of lost opportunities.[11] More specifically, Hamelin refutes the decapitation thesis by which his opponents account for the non-commercial aspects of life after the Conquest; a bourgeois class, he claims, would have had too strong a commitment to its colonial assets to return to France. Real control had always rested with extraterritorial interests, the state and the French bourgeoisie. For his part, Fernand Ouellet agrees that the Conquest brought no fundamental change to the colony, the capitalist mentality having never taken root because the colonial position in the French mercantile system had not promoted such a development.[12]

In opposition to Ouellet, however, W J Eccles has regarded the association with France in a more positive light, attributing the colonial achievement to the military forces, the capital, the direction, talent and administrative ability provided by the Crown.[13] In another analysis, Eccles claimed that the colony was the recipient of influences from two directions — the *ancien regime* and the Indians.[14] The former supplied the institutions which were humanitarian and paternalistic and generally well received, the latter many of the generally accepted attitudes which distinguished the colonials from Frenchmen. Looking at the dilemma of a bourgeois class from a slightly different perspective, Cameron Nish more or less accepts its existence. Nish identifies a man's function as the basis for determining his class.[15] Since the function of this class differed from that (one supposes) in the Anglo-American world because of its widespread interests in civil and military administration, the fur trade, and the seigneuries, Nish designates it *les bourgeois-gentilhommes de la Nouvelle-France*. What is significant about most of the foregoing literature — with the possible exception of those arguing along the lines set down by Hamelin and Ouellet — is its propensity to view New France as a society with certain germinal, identifiably liberalistic strains.

What will be argued here is the contrary point of view, that the predominant tendencies were highly conservative and that, if anything, whatever germinal liberalism once existed was eroded away. Colonial business was never permitted to define its profit objectives narrowly and to pursue them ruthlessly. Unlike the Anglo-American governments which evolved to defend the interests on the productive and credit side of the economy, the French authorities, still under the lingering effects of a medieval guild economy, were equally concerned with debtor and consumer rights. Furthermore, the state dictated the broad course of events which saw both religion and commerce, relatively speaking, as the declining forces and agriculture as the rising one. Had the colony limited its scope to the St Lawrence-Great Lakes region, a singular commercial value system may have developed. But the agricultural emphasis after 1663 and expansion into the Mississippi with its attendant military ethos meant no narrow and singular definition of commercial values. Indeed, despite the geographical expansion of commerce, mercantile values, in fact, weakened.

In contradistinction to European commerce in its late feudal genesis, the fur trade became an instrument of very exclusive colonial attitudes. The trader and the habitant, which as Guy Fregault has indicated, originally had a commercial connotation,[16] ceased to be one and the same. According to Eccles, the term "habitant" was conferred upon an individual who cleared four arpents of land and declared his willingness to settle permanently.[17] After the colony became a royal province, French merchants operating out of La Rochelle were induced, by potential profit, to establish direct links with the interior tribes. Eventually, wintering posts were organized in the Mississippi valley and west of Lake Superior. The habitant was no longer central to the fur trade and became more agrarian. Commercial opportunities were limited to relatively fewer members of the colonial population. Even the right to engage in commerce which was granted in 1685 to the Canadian *noblesse* — a mere handful of people — did not appreciably alter circumstances. Indeed, because of its internal diversity of function, the commercial community divided into "easterners" and "westerners" the former managing capital, fur processing, and marketing; the latter gathering and transporting fur from the interior.

Without the cohesion of a singular mercantile ethos, the commercial interests could hardly have dictated the colonial ideology. Besides, as Eccles has noted,[18] merchants continued to be attracted to the aristocratic ethos; financial success paradoxically eroded a possible liberal genesis by draining off the most competent commercial elements. Instead of offsetting the Indian-frontier influence — to use Eccles' terminology — commercial instincts submitted to an extraterritorial aristocratic-military ethos, itself declining in Europe. An influential factor in this, no doubt, was the weakening of colonial urban life. The initial fur trading posts had contained the entire population. Somewhat later, in the 1660's, half the colonial population lived in towns; just before the Conquest, only one quarter was still urban. Like the fur trade, city life was undergoing a *relative* decline from 1608 until 1760, its participating manpower measured against that of the total colonial economy. The initial commercial imperative was undermined by a colonial reversal of the urbanizing European demographic trend. The consequent capability of commerce to act as the predominant dispenser of colonial values was similarly limited.

In Europe a vibrant town life influenced the countryside, destroying feudal vestiges, but such did not occur along the St Lawrence, even after the Conquest. Linguistically French and

English merchants both acquired seigneuries and were subjected to highly conservative influences. When finally seigneurialism started to give way, it was not smashed by expanding, vital, indigenous liberalistic values but was crippled by the Imperial government, which in 1822 passed the Canada Trade Act to provide for voluntary changeovers from seigneurial to freehold tenure. This was followed by the Canada Tenures Act of 1825 which also kept commutations on a voluntary basis. Even so, the system limped on until 1854, inhibiting liberal propensities.

IV

Both land and monetary capital played a role in Canadian evolution quite different from their role in liberalizing societies. Not until the 1720s did France institute a fairly stable monetary system, after subjecting its colonials to fluctuating values because of monetary shortages and inflationary periods. Money had developed unpleasant associations in the colonial mentality because of its uncertain qualities, a factor which undoubtedly encouraged a lingering respect for feudalistic incentives. It was no accident, long after the Conquest, that so rural an area as Lower Canada never experienced a popular Jeffersonian-Jacksonian demand for easy credit. Of comparable significance was the observation made in the 1830s of "popular indifference" to the state of the currency with banks withdrawing good specie and circulating inferior.[19] Similarly, Upper Canada developed no popular sense of business economy. Whereas the major economic concern of the United States in the 1790s was the National Bank, Upper Canada became largely a barter economy. In neither province did money have congenial mercantile associations; in New France, it had derived in significant amounts from the illicit fur trade with the English colonies and, by way of governmental spending, from defence and public works. The latter also applied to Upper Canada where, in the 1820s, the colonial authorities resorted to debt financing and directed a substantial amount of revenue to a few costly projects. Both financing and spending were exclusive, not popular activities.

Land was to the American west what money had been to late feudal Europe, a relatively common commodity whose popular use imposed common values throughout society. Initially, the American Republic was founded by a leftward Jeffersonian respect for very tangible assets such as real estate and a somewhat more rightward Federalist concern for assets of a less concrete nature such as stocks, bonds, mortgages, and fluid capital. After the War of 1812 the north-east moved leftwards towards western style materialism. The investment of eastern capital in industry as opposed to the earlier emphasis on commerce meant that eastern investments in factories, machinery, and real estate were assuming a more concrete nature. Despite a lingering northeastern respect for fluid capital, the gap between a lesser eastern materialism and a greater western type almost disappeared. With the expansion of the singular northern value system into the south by force of arms several decades later, the liberalization process was completed in the United States.

Canada has never established a comparable singular value system based on civil rights and the sanctity of private property. Upper Canada was originally peopled by the Loyalists who were monarchical and anti-American. Then, curiously enough, the Federalist reaction of 1787 induced de facto Jeffersonian migrations into the province. These de facto Jeffersonians equated the Republic to reaction and reinforced the original Upper Canadian anti-Americanism. The War of 1812 added another conservative dimension. Just as American liberal nationalism grew in intensity from eastern to western states, so did a corresponding opposite sentiment characterize the British American colonies. New Brunswick which bordered Federalist anti-war states exhibited no abiding hatred of the United States and the liberalism which it symbolized but Upper Canada which suffered the full weight of War Hawk fury was quite the contrary. Nor did Upper Canadian animosities cease after the War of 1812. Local colonial authority became deeply committed to the elimination of landholders of American origin. At issue were the related questions of citizenship and right of representation in the House of Assembly. Although the Chief Justice of England had ruled in 1824 that those who had remained in the United States after 1783 had lost their right to retain and transmit British citizenship and to inherit real estate in the Empire, in 1826 the Imperial government made naturalization dependent upon seven years' residence in the province. Thus, the provincial authority had actually attempted to infringe property and civil rights. Although the Imperial government rectified the situation, it robbed the populace of an indigenous opportunity to sanctify rights in private property as had happened earlier in the Anglo-American world.

Despite its proximity to the dynamic and liberal Jeffersonian west, other factors engendered illiberalism in Upper Canada. Upper Canadian land developed relatively static associations. The oath of loyalty neutralized whatever Jeffersonian popularism did arrive with American immigrants. Nor did the expansionary aspects of Jeffersonianism have any genuine application because of the physical limitations of the available amount of provincial real estate. After the Louisiana Purchase of 1803, the American west again became the logical attraction for committed Jeffersonians. The frontier, in short, never acted as a social leveller and liberalizer in Upper Canada. Like New France where much land had conservative associations by way of seigneurial tenure and the large tracts held by religious orders, that of Upper Canada was equally constrained by privately held Tory tracts whose sole objective was speculation and the Clergy and Crown Reserves, all of which discouraged popular development.

What made the social impact of land different in Canada and the United States was that, in the latter instance, land fostered a dynamic individualism that came to be legally enshrined. In the Canada of New France a western expansionary dynamism had existed but was associated, not with agriculture but with the fur trade. Unlike American western land, fur was not a commodity which tangibly symbolized intangible values and functioned as a transmission belt to the colonial masses. As a slowly expansive force, land meshed with the existing representative institutions in the Thirteen Colonies by providing the basis for increasingly popular enfranchisement. While cleared land was a productive agricultural investment, fur had no comparable quality of capital appreciation and lacked the capacity of an attractive investment whose mere possession inculcated liberal values. As a staple trading commodity, fur became the expansive agent of strategic military considerations dictated by Paris and, as such, encouraged an exclusive, elitist social structure which persisted after the Conquest, while American western land created an egalitarian basis for the evolution of a popular society.

V

In the Anglo-American societies, the "directional" evolutionary tendency toward an indigenous popular leadership seems to have flowed considerably from economic considerations, whereas in Canada leadership has been, in a manner of speaking, the recipient of political and social considerations. Although opinions abound concerning the Upper Canadian Family Compact and its Tory allies, it seems not to have emerged from economic activity. One commentator, S F Wise, has observed that a vast governmental bureaucracy based on patronage and the "clientage" system came into existence by 1812 to satisfy the requirements of the conservative imperative.[20] The provincial constitution was "doubled" in the sense that it outwardly adhered to the structure of the British colonial establishment while inwardly the governmental apparatus and that of the Tory "party" were virtually identical. The "party" consisted of a quasi-official coalition of the central and local elites which distributed honours to those sufficiently deserving. An "in" group developed — later called the Family Compact — which was based far less on merit than on personal relationships and adherence to proper views.

For Wise it seems evident that economic considerations were not central to the Compact's existence. William Kilbourn asserts that the Compact was an "aristocracy on the make" and wished to obtain the characteristic privileges.[21] If this be true, then its intention of setting the standard in morals and religion and its general paternalism did not equip it for liberalistic endeavours. This is not to say that its membership, as Kilbourn readily admits, did not contain those on the periphery of entrepreneurial activity — a few bank directors, but mainly merchants and land agents. Such were pretty small stuff. Gerald M Craig has claimed that the Compact, which was really a series of local compacts, drew heavily on second generation loyalists and immigrants from Britain and their sons. Its membership regarded itself as part of the British nation.[22] Consequently, for these people the Empire remained more important than one of its parts and the Compact, under such circumstances, could hardly have functioned as an indigenous provincial leadership. According to Craig, the Compact tended to see governmental authority as a derivative of monarchical principle, history and religion. That encouraged dependence.

Robert Saunders has divided the Compact into an "elite of office" and an "elite of power". Between 1820 and 1837, eight persons were identified in the latter, although not all were simultaneously present; this group, claims Saunders, was the centre of everything — government, the Bank of Upper Canada, the Welland Canal and all major enterprises.[23] Basically, the Compact was a vast interlinking association of office holders who were admitted to their positions by the power elite. Pursuit of commercial and business opportunity was, if anything, peripheral to Compact activity rather than central.

There seems to be general agreement that the leadership and society of Upper Canada were not parallel to the Anglo-American. Leadership was not, in Upper Canada, the logical extension of popular values inculcated by the educating force of land and capital. The economic interests of the Compact seem to have developed from their socio-political functions. The Compact and Tories eventually became involved in the Bank of Upper Canada and the Welland Canal Company but these projects were so crucial to provincial wellbeing that any participant could expect governmental intervention if serious difficulty developed. As H G J Aitken makes clear, the Welland Canal Company profited from its Compact associations, both legislatively and financially.[24] So too was the Bank of Upper Canada's connection to the authorities very close: by 1831 twenty-five percent of the shares were government owned and four out of eleven directors had been appointed by the Lieutenant-Governor. For the Compact and Tories, the risk factors were less than the necessary minimum to inculcate the judicious attitudes of a competent business class. Robert Saunders makes a further telling point; in rejecting earlier views of a business-Compact inter-relationship, he ascertains a steady decline in commercial pursuits in the two decades before 1837. Saunders is speculating — somewhat along the lines of Kilbourn — that the Compact was acquiring a quasi-aristocratic contempt for business and money-making.

Without liberalization of the economy, the power structure remained quite exclusive and dependent on the executive branch. A cancellation of public works projects in 1836 by the Lieutenant-Governor dislocated the entire economy. The uncertainties of arbitrary state interference in the economy which the English Puritans and their mercantile successors and the American revolutionaries had resolved was still open to question in the province. Upper Canada continued to function as a pre-mercantile illiberal community. Nor did the Upper Canadian left emulate the Anglo-American liberals and offer the prospect of relief. In revolutionary Russia of a later day Lenin promised the peasantry land which, at least, obtained peasant neutrality if not open loyalty. In France the revolutionaries had similarly captured widespread support by redistributing the landed wealth of the Catholic Church. So too had Henry VIII in England. One of the attractions of the American Revolution involved opening western land to settlement.

The would-be Upper Canadian revolutionary, William Lyon Mackenzie, approximated, by intent, such leftward gestures. In November 1837 a broadside contained promises of free gifts of Clergy Reserves land, Church of England Glebe Lots, and Canada Company land to all those settled on them. Mackenzie also promised to give fifty-seven rectories to the people.[25] Two points may be made in respect to this program; first, as it aimed to benefit relatively few people, it was really a very exclusive gesture, not a popular one. Secondly, it was philosophically unsound: any infringement of property rights was a denial of the liberal philosophy of the type of social system which Mackenzie was otherwise expounding; it was vaguely reminiscent of the extreme, leftward, Daniel Shays' type of attitude which the Americans, themselves, had rejected. Seizure of land called into question the very principles which those who stood to benefit from the initial seizure would certainly wish applied in their defence. Mackenzie's program actually worked against a broad base of popular revolutionary support.

Although the Lieutenant-Governor of Upper Canada, John Graves Simcoe, had intended the Upper Province to become a "little England", the development both of its ruling class and its would-be revolutionaries illustrates, not a liberalizing ideology deriving largely from economic considerations, but something quite different.

VI

In Lower Canada, there has been a tendency to trace the Rebellion of 1837 to the growth of a "popular" and/or "democratic" party. Few habitants had voted before 1800 and, when they did, generally supported the governmental candidates. On the other hand, non-popular manifestations had also grown in significance since the Conquest: the old institution of the captains of militia had fallen into disuse by the 1820s leaving their rivals for local influence, the curés, predominant. Since the Recollets and Jesuits had originally provided the teachers, illiteracy had become more prevalent after 1763. By 1784, less than twenty per cent of the population could read. This situation was reversed in the decade before 1837: between 1828 and 1832, there was a pronounced rise in the student population. But the "popular" party, based as it was almost totally on the linguistically French agrarian community, represented a very narrow, largely ethnic-economic imperative. Such exclusiveness, even if it constitutes the majority interest, is not popular in the same sense as liberalism which acts as a social leveller and encourages common values beyond the limitations of language and religion. Such a conservative concept of community life was really an obstacle to revolution.

Another indication of this non-popular tendency may be found in the concept of leadership indigenous to the St Lawrence community. The habitant mentality had always associated leadership with alien, extraterritorial institutions, especially the state, both French and British, and, to a lesser degree, the Roman Catholic Church. A local, colonial and personality-based leadership was largely unknown: Louis Joseph Papineau and the Lower Canadian rebels of 1837 may have been native sons but that was actually an obstacle to their effectiveness in a society where final authority had always been abstract and distant. The Conquest had introduced the additional barrier of language which associated the left with English qualities which, understandably, the French Canadian tended to reject in a body.

Given the very nature of the psychological and linguistic inhibitions, only individuals, not the whole community, were able to cross this frontier of highly divergent values. The few who did develop a respect for leftward principles found that it cost them empathy with the habitant masses because the latter had remained psychologically unable to function under a popular style of leadership. One must never forget that popular liberalization as it developed in Europe was not originally articulated. One simply interacted with the increasingly important monetary economy and the classes which were promoting it. The resulting trans-mission of values was gradual. Not until the Glorious Revolution did Locke articulate what was already accepted. The French Canadians had never experienced a comparable re-education in their everyday lives. Three centuries of liberalizing socio-political evolution separated the revolutionary leadership of 1837 from its intended followers. Nor did the immediate contributing causes of the 1837 Rebellion help alleviate this situation.

The deep mercantile depression of 1836 and 1837, whose leftward economic style the revolutionaries symbolized — although they would have emphatically denied it — could hardly have appeared as a viable alternative to the habitants, already in despair over the wheat economy's collapse mainly brought on by natural disasters. As in 1760 and 1774, the leftward economic style came to involve negative connotations which, specifically, seemed to offer no solutions to the problems of 1837. The total result reinforced the long standing sense of antipathy to the popular left, especially since its spokesmen, the Papineau rebels, were militarily discredited in 1837 and virtually disappeared from the socio-political spectrum. They had, of course, been deceived by thinking that the casual factor operating in 1837 was similar to that of 1774. But neither the actions of the Imperial government nor the taxation-representation issue was similar. The Ten Resolutions which broke the financial impasse may have been an "intolerable" gesture but they were not harmful to the habitants as fundamentally as the Intolerable Acts of 1774 had been to the very existence of the Boston merchants and the western farmers. In the absence of a genuine popular issue to mobilize *active* mass support, the victory of the state over the revolutionaries was a foregone conclusion and paralleled that of the sister province.

VII

The legalities by which liberal societies defend their citizens against arbitrary state power never developed in Canada. Post-revolutionary Anglo-American political philosophy associated four concepts — private property and its defence with good (ie local) government, political leadership, and human rationality. In Canada in 1837, defence of the state by propertied interests denied the traditional Anglo-American evolution toward liberalism with its desire for local political independence from imposed authority. Tory rebelliousness in 1849 similarly denied the propertied quest for order and rationality. Nothing so clearly indicates Tory alienation from the latter as the destruction of the Canadian parliament buildings which were elsewhere the symbol of liberal values triumphant. The Tory riot had aimed to halt the Imperial disengagement from Canada and to stop the advent of responsible government. It was established, significantly, by the Rebellion Losses Bill which compensated not only the victims but also the destroyers of property in the Rebellion of 1837. Circumstance had transformed the Tories — those who would ordinarily be the mercantile allies of liberalism — into its *de facto* foes in Canada.

This explains why the mercantile interests could later so readily ally with the Bleus of Quebec despite the latter's association with a Roman Catholic revival which began in the 1840s. Often regarded only as pragmatic politics, ideological empathy did play a large role. The strengthening of Catholicism represented, in a sense, a continuing negation of the Anglo-American tradition which, from the thirteenth century, had aimed to curb such influences. The eventual Ultramontane victory in Quebec over the Gallicans rejuvenated the emphasis on extraterritorial papal authority, attempted to re-establish the primacy of the Church over the state which resulted in a more vigorous brand of "pulpit politics" in a land with representative institutions, and brought about a renewed tendency toward social corporatism. The Conservative Party through which the Bleus and their mercantile allies functioned became the instrument of illiberalism.

The Conservative Party and the Confederation to which it eventually gave rise had been created during a period of relative moderation. The radicals and their liberalistic claims had been discredited in 1837 and, during the period of Imperial retrench- ment which started in the late 1840s, the Canadian Tories with their intense Imperial loyalties were replaced by the Conservatives who represented a somewhat more localistic emphasis. But, quite clearly, there was no fundamental commitment to a singular value system, liberal or otherwise. Unlike the United States whose Constitution provided the federal jurisdiction with police powers to defend private property, there was no comparable association in Canada, partly, no doubt, because of Bleu concerns over Quebec's unique body of civil law. In the British North America Act the "peace, order, and good government" clause of Section 91 which defines federal authority has conflicted with the "property and civil rights" clause of Section 92 which defines provincial power. Nor, even in its provincial context, did "property and civil rights" accord with liberal principles, for the former were not stated as inviolate and intrinsic limitations to governmental power; "property and civil rights" opened the way for an enormous expansion of provincial authority directed, in fact, at the federal government and, potentially, against the population which lacked constitutional assurances. The late nineteenth century's judicial victories of "property and civil rights" over "peace, order and good government" associated concepts of civil rights, property, and provincial authority with an evolutionary trend contrary to the Anglo-American. Instead of aiding the erection of a popular state structure, "property and civil rights" helped undermine Confederation and, by logical extension, the very concept of Canada. A certain amount of evidence has, in fact, been accumulated which indicates that the state in Canada, especially at the provincial level, has never been inhibited about infringing private property rights. And, even more significantly, the federal government has been impotent in halting the process.[26]

Understandably, the Canadian public has developed no great empathy for the federal authority. Its association with generally recognized and accepted "Canadian" values did not materialize. Perhaps the most commonly recognized federal function in Canada has been associated with potentially unlimited taxation which, of course, places Ottawa in a contrary role to the American government whose *raison d'être* has been defence of property and civil rights. Taxation and its restriction to the other enumerated powers of Section 91 of the British North America Act, except during periods of "national" crises which the Judicial Committee in 1922 defined as war and famine, have substantially limited Ottawa.

Nor did transcontinentalism aid the emergence of liberalism in Canada as it did in the United States. According to Donald Creighton, a native Canadian drive to continentalism existed and was strengthened by two external forces, British insistence and American pressure. Acquisition of the west was a pragmatic response. For Innis, expansion was linked with the necessity of organizing the continental interior for the trade in staples. Reconstitution and expansion were engineered, according to Innis, by the dominant interests in business and government which overlapped considerably. It is being suggested here, along somewhat different lines, that the Coalition of 1864 impregnated the Conservative Party with tendencies antithetical to its Canadian interests. Canada did not simply react pragmatically to American pressure; the latter served as a direct inspiration for transcontinental expansion. Just as the Republican Party of Lincoln had absorbed notions of Manifest Destiny from its "free soil" wing on the frontier, so too did the Conservatives receive the same concept by way of the Grits in the 1864 Coalition. Concepts related to liberal principles from the United States were thus implanted in the constitutional fabric of Confederation, especially western transcontinentalism. The Grits, in effect, relinquished the concept of Manifest Destiny to the Conservatives who, by 1873, had successfully implemented its expansionary aspects. Unfortunately, Conservativism lacked the popular cohesive materialism of genuine Manifest Destiny and the means to transmit it to the masses. What was lacking, of course, was the sheer ingraining power of land along a slowly receding frontier. Without a well defined imperative that was fundamental to the Canadian community, the Conservatives were hardly in a position to "Canadianize" the west — or, for that matter, the Maritimes. That the Conservative Party attracted support by the pragmatic method of subsidy and patronage is indicative of its failure to constitute a national image such as the liberal American which had created an ongoing sense of unfulfilled idealism dedicated to the emancipation of Man from the negatives of his condition. While the very existence of Canada is being increasingly questioned, the unifying universality of (Anglo-)American liberalism persists still, proclaiming not what men are but rather what they should be.

VIII

In the United States, reform movements had been successful to the degree that they were associated with the liberal mainstream of American life. By way of contrast, reform in Canada has come to involve three possibilities. First, if reform had genuinely liberal pretensions as it did in 1837, then it also had ideologically alien (ie Anglo-American; non-Canadian) connotations. This automatically and paradoxically depopularized the reform movement and rendered it void. Second have been reform movements so mild as to raise the question of the validity of classing them as reforms. The activities of the Bleus and the Liberals fell into this area. Third, the most recent instrument of rhetorical reform to appear in Canada has been the New Democratic Party. Irrespective of the theory involved, reform is only significant in its functional application. Insofar as New Democracy exists, there is an enormous discrepancy between theory and reality. The first of the foregoing points has, of course, been examined in detail so that what follows will be devoted to the second and third points.

Gad Horowitz,[27] possibly reacting to the necessary economic-political emphasis of the staples thesis, has offered an alternative and ideological interpretation of Canadian history, an interpretation based on a curious conservative-socialistic rendering of the liberal or pan-North American school. If Horowitz did react to the staples thesis, then he did so by ignoring it; if he also reacted to the Americanizing tendencies in the liberal school, then he did so by stressing the conservative, tory, and feudal dimension which has found its unique (North) American ideological expression in Canada but not in the United States. Canadian Liberalism, Horowitz claims, has been tainted by toryism, whereas American liberalism has been monolithic and pure. For the liberal school, the relatively conservative ideological characteristics which have set Canada off from the United States have generally been regarded as aberrations; for Horowitz, however, these tory characteristics meant that Canada had largely replicated the fundamental ideological spectrum of Europe. What has distinguished Canada from Europe has been the relative weight of each constituent ideology. The tory element which had left the nascent United States had never been significant there, but its arrival in Canada after 1776 meant that toryism came to be a much stronger force in a land which, like its American neighbour, was, nonetheless, still essentially liberal.

The tory element with its communitarian emphasis, according to Horowitz, provided Canada with the non-liberal elements which have persistently accounted, unlike the United States, for the uniquely Canadian political mix — a centre Liberal Party tempered by rightward tory-inspired Conservativism and by leftward socialism, the latter mingling tory communitarianism with liberalistic notions of rational egalitarianism. For Horowitz, what has distinguished Canada has been the power of its political centre, Liberalism, which has resisted the lure of leftward reform common to Europe. In Europe, socialism has virtually eliminated the liberal centre as a significant force. In the United States, because only liberalism survived the Revolution and because no comparative ideological standard has existed within the Republic, the Americans have unwittingly denied their classical liberalism in the recent and varied interventionist programmes of the welfare state.

There is much to be said of the structure imposed by Horowitz and some specifics will shortly follow. Generally, one might ask why Horowitz insists on utilizing the traditional ideological system, especially when he notes the curious disappearance in Europe of centre liberalism and the strength of the European left and right and also when he notes the astounding similarity of Canadian Conservativism and socialism. What one finds in Horowitz' ideological system is the relentlessly imposed ideology of historical inquiry, itself, the sheer necessity of leftward progress and the mind-set which derives directly from it. Both in Europe and in Canada, it surely makes sense to associate the largely rhetorical and theoretical left which arose in the late eighteenth century and in the nineteenth with the traditional functional right. What the socialistic left did absorb, arriving as it did after the advent of liberalism with its attractive emancipating concepts, were the *notions* of justice, environmental mastery, respect for science, and a profound sense of necessary progress.

The point is this: the liberal dimension *in socialism* has mostly consisted of rhetoric and theory whereas the substance has been tory because the latter has been in accord with the indigenous functional development of Europe/Canada. As for the United States, its genesis may have prompted a distinctive tory quality in Canada but one should not casually draw analogies between post-revolutionary America and Europe/Canada because the 1776 Revolution *totally* detached America from the European ideological spectrum: the generally held conceptual notions based on the equation of progressive liberal modernity to the universal left, although recognized in a liberal-linear historical system, have not been truly applicable. Although Horowitz has not been cognizant of it, his ideological perception has done much to upset the conventional linear progressivist concept of history. On this point and another — the question of whether Canadian Liberalism has been, in fact, liberal — one may organize both a reply to Horowitz and structure a re-examination of reform and liberalism in Canada.

Horowitz claims that the loyalists and the Family Compact did not represent British toryism (which he equates to feudalism) but pre-revolutionary American Whiggery with a tory touch. This is a rejection of the traditional view of Upper (ie English) Canada which, according to Horowitz, was that English Canada was founded by British tories. Their purpose had been to build a society which would not be liberal like the American but conservative like the British. What Horowitz fails to perceive is that both British society and American society once may have been fundamentally liberal, so that the choices that he proposes never really existed. What Horowitz seems further to have ignored is the *directional* feature of Upper Canadian ideological evolution. If the loyalists arrived in the province from a basically liberal society and, in so doing, strengthened their tory tendencies, then, quite evidently, their initial evolutionary thrust in Upper Canada was rightward. Utilizing Louis Hartz' concept of ideological "congealment", Horowitz places this moment quite late in English Canadian development; if this be true, then Horowitz' alleged liberalism with a tory touch must have remained unstable for an equal time period, since a society's definitive ideology is not supposed to occur until "congealment". In other words, to reverse Horowitz' thesis, one cannot be certain, in the absence of congealment, that Upper Canada did not become a tory society with a liberal tinge, or even a purely tory society.

According to Horowitz, toryism with its stress on monarchy, elitism, deference to authority, and state direction of the economy was most pronounced in the Conservative Party which remained, nonetheless, essentially liberal. What such a perspective neglects is the fact that the predominant influence in Canadian Conservatism from the 1840s until the 1890s was French Canadian and, irrespective of Horowitz' theory of English Canadian liberalism tinged with toryism, the complexion of the Conservative Party's actions and activities — its functional translation — was *quite* tory. Speaking generally of the nineteenth century and earlier especially in the Anglo-American world, one may define liberalizing reform as popular limitation to the role of the state by the popular erection of mechanisms to defend private property and civil rights from the state above and the masses beneath, and, in the broadest rhetorical terms, the espousal of "liberty" and individualism. None of the Bleu-dominated Conservative Party reforms involved the foregoing. The Rebellion Losses Bill did shift power from the Imperial authority to the Canadian legislature, but there its exercise fell to the Bleus who were further to the right than the

Imperial Parliament. The Guarantee Act of 1849 assisted railway builders to raise capital by providing provincial guarantees and by permitting municipalities to provide capital; the University of Toronto became a secular institution; the Court of Chancery was established to simplify the legal system; and the rule of primogeniture was ended in 1850. Nothing in any of this fundamentally attacked the illiberal foundations of Bleu principles which their political allies dared not test.

After the Bleu-Conservative alliance of 1854, another series of "reforms" occurred. The Municipal Act of 1855 provided for elective institutions for local government. Between 1857 and 1866, the highly chaotic system of justice in Canada East was systematized. The Legislative Council was made elective in 1857, which could be interpreted as a democratic gesture but was a conservative one, since the upper house could function, thereafter, more dynamically to check the lower one in the name of the public interest. The Bleus were less aggressive than the Rouges and the Grits so that a potentially more restrictive upper house was directed against the Reformers. Again, the Bleu position remained inviolate. Even when the Liberals as the heirs of the Rouge and Clear Grit traditions took power after the Pacific Scandal of 1873, no genuine and fundamental erosion of state power occurred. The governor general was brought more firmly under the control of the prime minister and cabinet but this was more a continuing shift of power within the Imperial state structure rather than a popular gesture. The Elections Act of 1874 provided for voting in a single day which undoubtedly influenced the fortunes of political parties but not the state. The establishment of the Royal Military College in 1874 to train a professional officer corps for the militia strengthened the authoritarian tendency by providing its instrument of enforcement. The Prohibition Act of 1878 increased governmental power by providing for regulation of sales and consumption of spirits. Even the Dominion Franchise Act of 1885 seems to have been more of a simple concession from above than a popular achievement. The point is this: the Canadian concept of reform — or what has passed for reform — has been markedly different from the national reforming liberalism of the Anglo-American world.

There had been, at various times, an intensification of leftward political pressure, and the Bleus consistently negated it, as in
1854, with the creation of the Conservative Party, and in 1864 with
the Grand Coalition. The Conservative Party had been the
product of a new alignment which the Bleus sought when the
Upper Canadian Reformers ceased to be useful collaborators in
the lower house. True to the principle established by Lafontaine,
the Bleus began to seek a new linguistically English ally because
their own linguistic bloc was dividing and creating the more
liberal Rouge Party. Neither the Bleus nor the Rouges had the
option of remaining aloof from alignments: this would have
isolated them and caused that purely ethnic polarization intended
by Lord Durham more than a decade earlier, with all its attendant
consequences. After 1849, the Montreal business interests recognized the economic benefits of associating with Bleu voting power;
so too, did the Canada West Conservatives who also needed such
an ally in the legislature to resist the growing Clear Grit appeal.
The resulting trade-off — internal improvements and acceptance
of (ethnic) pluralism — was agreeable to all concerned, because no
popular (anti-exclusive) gestures were involved.

Mounting leftward pressure again became intolerable by the
early 1860s when political deadlock revealed that the Act of Union
of 1840 no longer provided a viable constitution, involving as it
did equal representation for both Canadas. Perhaps the serious
business of securing a reconstitution based on representation by
population started with the election of 1857. This election ended
Bleu adherence to the principal of "double majority" which had
dictated their basic political method for a decade. The possibility
of the dominant Bleu interest from Canada East working with the
dominant interest of Canada West was not feasible because the
latter section fell under Reform influence which desired reconstitution.[28] The Bleus refused to hazard such an event because their
position under the Union was relatively secure. But by mid 1864 a
definite equilibrium had developed in the legislature between
those who wished to reconstitute the Union and those who did not.
Both methods by which political parties had functioned under the
Act of Union had become impossible; the majority parties from
each section could not work together by virtue of differing views

on the validity of the 1840 constitution and the majority-minority political combination had become too evenly balanced for effective government. Both principles were utilized briefly in the Grand Coalition to break the deadlock and to provide a solution: the Bleu majority of Canada East allied with both the majority and the minority of Canada West, the George Brown Grit Reformers and the John A Macdonald Conservatives, respectively. From this position, the Bleus were able to modify the leftward reform thrust sufficiently that it did Bleu interests no fundamental injury. What permitted the Conservative Party to accede to the Grit-sponsored Coalition was its very pluralism. Quite obviously, Horowitz correctly ascertained that Canadian Conservativism was no liberal monolith but he substantially neglected the Bleu dimension (which was pluralistic, feudal, "tory") of early Conservatism. This dimension seems to have been the Party's predominant *functional* ideological aspect, its occasional liberalistic rhetoric notwithstanding.

In joining the Grand Coalition, both Bleus and Grits must have been partly inspired by American examples in the early 1860s. The Grits had wished to remove from Canada West the disabilities imposed by Bleu political power in the Assembly, as had the Lincolnian Republicans wished to check the Democrats with their strong southern support in Congress. The success of the Republican-Free Soil east-west axis in "correcting" the previous political "imbalance" in the Republic could hardly have passed unnoticed in Canada by 1864. The Grand Coalition also took the form of an east-west axis involving a party with business pursuits and one with agrarian interests. So long as the Bleus went along with the Grand Coalition they could check disadvantageous initiatives from the Grits; the American Democrats, by way of contrast, could not effect similar results because the Southern Secession had left the federal government at the mercy of the Republicans. Like the Democrats, the Bleus were on the defensive and the lesson was obvious — participate in the Coalition to influence the outcome or face the possibility of a severe reversal.

Horowitz has referred to Canadian Liberalism as the "triumphant centre" but, unlike the liberalism of the American Democratic Party, Canadian Liberalism has been rendered "impure" by contacts with toryism and, more recently, with socialism. Canadian Liberalism has been, consequently, less individualistic, less popular and democratic, has adopted state intervention in the economy, and has even accepted monarchy, a feudal survival. Simply put, Canadian Liberalism, in the European tradition, has constituted a Party which opposed the class parties, as Horowitz would say, of the right and the left (by which Horowitz means, in the conventional sense, socialism) by espousing "national" unity. What has afforded this opportunity has been the obscure and ambivalent language of Canadian Liberalism which has permitted it to avoid rigorous self definition. Canada has been, Horowitz assures us, the only society in which Liberal reform has faced the challenge of socialism and has emerged victorious.

Horowitz' most significant weakness is his failure to deal, at least minimally, with the French Canadian influence on Liberalism after the 1896 election. Just as the Bleus had checked the Conservatives from instituting a genuine liberal reform in the four decades previously, so did their legacy similarly negate the Liberals. Canadian Liberalism succeeded in the Canadian political context precisely because it was *not* a centre party of the traditional Western type but one which, in accordance with the Bleu legacy, shifted rightward into the comfortable, attractive, and essentially Canadian territory of tory-socialism. Canada may have become more (politically and socially) democratic in this century but it did so without liberalization (ie without challenging the concept of exclusive community interests so basic to the Liberal Party's dominant voting bloc). The Liberal Party triumphed in 1896, ultimately, because it moved into the illiberal Canadian mainstream and thereafter drew off tory and socialist votes, while, on the other hand, remaining secure in its pseudo-liberal appeal with the absence of a truly liberal party in Canada. Genuine Canadian liberalism, whatever its possible strength, was clearly checked by Liberal ambivalence. The English Canadian "tory touch" (to utilize Horowitz' terminology) and the French Canadian voting bloc have remained functionally supreme.

If liberalism, as Horowitz has claimed, has involved equality of opportunity, which meant use of state power in the nineteenth century to destroy monopolies and the creation of a welfare floor in the twentieth, the latter in Canada, most probably, had very little to do with liberalism and much to do with political democracy. There has been an unfortunate tendency in Canada as elsewhere to regard political democracy as a necessary adjunct to liberalism. In the Anglo-American world this is quite valid for democracy did largely derive from the other. But the attempt to apply a similar necessary relationship to Canada has been unfounded because the democratic achievement in Canada was not at all incompatible with the traditional rightward forces. The pre-Conquest French regime had been devoted to a measure of social justice based on medieval concepts which favoured the consumer and debtor rather than the producer, creditor, and the owner of property. Nor had the latter interests ever checked the state in Canada: its traditional exercise of power to restrain economically predominant but numerically limited interests has not been an alien concept. Concession of the benefits of democracy were also encouraged by the indigenous tradition of a broad franchise based on relatively cheap land. The extraterritorial nature of the Canadian state also contributed to the growth of democracy. As the Anglo-American world liberalized and democratized, resistance by the state in Canada to democracy increasingly became morally indefensible. By a process of Anglo-American osmosis, Canada achieved liberalism's superficial outgrowth, political democracy. The point is, of course, that Canadian democracy arose exclusive of popular liberal reform and that the later welfare state, too, arrived in Canada by way of political democracy but not by way of an essential liberalism tempered by tory paternalism as Horowitz seems to believe.

An earlier commentator on the shortcomings of the liberal tradition in Canada, F H Underhill, has pointed out the Canadian failure to intellectualize and to articulate an indigenous liberalism.[29] This contributed, according to Underhill, to the over-all weakness of reform in such an area as the Canadian failure to control domination of government by business interests in the late nineteenth century as did the Americans. Underhill, although aware of the intense anti-liberal forces at work in Canada, seems never to have contemplated their total ideological victory. There had been no basic attack on business as an exclusive interest because all Canadian interests have been exclusive ones. In contradistinction to the American socio-ideology which was a levelling and a homogenizing force, that of Canada has been specifically engineered to preserve existing entrenched and exclusive interests, whether French Canadian ethnicity or Anglo-dominated staples-based big business. The acceptance by the Liberal Party of this fundamental *raison d'être* of Canadian society has meant that (the Anglo-American style of) liberal reform has been virtually impossible, irrespective of the advent of political democracy in Canada.

Socialism in Canada contributed to Canada's non-American distinctiveness, for Horowitz, in two ways: Canadian socialism has been a significant, legitimate political force; it was British, worldly, non Marxist. British immigrants to Canada, Horowitz claims, engaged in direct (socialistic) value transmission from the old world to the congenial, somewhat tory, ideological atmosphere in Canada. In the United States, the true (ie socialistic European/Canadian) left had no opportunity for a legitimate existence because its tory ideological *raison d'être* did not survive 1776; those who attempted to introduce socialism after the Revolution were at variance with the monolithic, post-revolutionary liberal reality by reason of their ethnic origin, German, and their ideological preference, Marxism. The consequent reform mechanism in the United States has been the liberal Democratic wing which encouraged the interventionist welfare system. In Canada with more than one legitimate ideology, according to Horowitz, the situation has been quite distinctive with the Liberals responding to the socialistic left by absorbing its programmes and, thereby, neutralizing the socialistic chance for power but not eliminating the persistent legitimacy of the ideology, itself.

The "tory touch" which characterized alleged Canadian liberalism has meant, in Horowitz' system, that ideas not totally compatible with liberalism would at least be tolerated in English Canada. Because English Canada was not monolithically liberal like the United States, English Canada has been as willing to dabble in socialism as in toryism. Horowitz has stated that socialism and toryism constitute, respectively, left (that is, left of liberalism) and right concepts. But surely, based on Horowitz' own evidence and line of thought, both merit a conceptually rightward treatment, the socialistic strain — irrespective of certain liberalistic elements — merely being the "reverse side" of the class emphasis prevalent in toryism. For a society to be tory (or "feudal" according to the Hartz-Horowitz system) is to be communitarian, divided, non-homogeneous, pluralistic. From a conceptual perspective, it is easier and more practical to account for Canadian politics with toryism and socialism rightward and Liberalism somewhat leftward — but not so far leftward, obviously, as American liberalism.

What has distinguished socialism from toryism has been the modern egalitarian rhetoric and theory of socialism which did, after all, arise in the modern (liberal) period. By placing homogeneous societies and parties to the left and those less so to the right according to relative diversity, a more perfect conceptual comprehension is possible than occurs with a left to right graph extending from socialism, through Liberalism, and Conservativism (with its tory strain). Horowitz, himself, puzzled over the aberration of "radicalism" and "leftism" which has characterized orthodox Conservatives, a situation which amounted to "red toryism" in some instances. Horowitz concluded — and rightly so — that the aberration was based on a close affinity of socialism and toryism. Under these circumstances, the illiberal right may be said to contain both socialists and tories, a fact which also helps account for the fundamental irrationality and diversity of the right. This rightward position may explain why the New Democratic and Conservative Parties have been, by definition, less "national" and more exclusive, limited, "provincial" than the Liberals.

New Democracy has proposed to alleviate economic and social inequalities by more generous methods of redistributing wealth. But, if one lesson is to be drawn from the Anglo-American constitutional experiment, then certainly it is that current concepts of justice and civil rights, although largely imported into Canada, are elsewhere grounded in, and evolved out of, the erection of safeguards to secure one's private assets against the state and the masses. The New Democrats, by disassociating social justice from its popular materialistic foundations, are attempting an impossible task. The major mechanism in this process is to be the interventionist state, a situation which closely approximates the traditional tory economic instrument. New Democracy, like Conservativism and Liberalism, is very Canadian: all are quite illiberal. By convention, reform has always been associated with allegedly leftward instruments, liberal Democrats in monolithic America and socialists in Europe. But in Canada liberalism was illegitimate and socialistic rhetoric was without substance. The ideological spectrum was not as complete as Horowitz believed, but was only a rightward fragment. Canada has had, consequently, no native capacity for genuine reform.

IX

Gad Horowitz, who sees Canadian uniqueness — the country's distinct identity — as a manifestation of a liberal society with a tory strain, has brought the liberal school of Canadian history to an ideological position very close to that of the conservative liberal school. Admittedly, Horowitz is a professed socialist, but in his historical writing, he sees Canada as a fundamentally liberal extension of the United States and in that sense may be said to write in the liberal school of Canadian history. The method by which Horowitz arrives at his view is quite distinct from the use of the staples perspective, with its British and European associations, favoured by the conservative liberal school. Yet one must ask if, ideologically, anything essential remains to be accomplished by either school. Glenn Porter has noted in a recent article the failure to write integrating histories, Canadian historiography having been, of late, characterized by a sense of drift and disunity.[30] This is, of course, indicative of the major problem confronting Canada itself.

The absence of integrating liberalism in Canada is extremely significant. It has been claimed that the Canadian mosaic which recognizes group diversity is more tolerant than American liberalism with its stress on individualism and homogeneity. Most probably, Canada has not been any more tolerant than the United States. Rather, the tolerance has differed in type: the United States has been tolerant within the context of liberal variation; Canada has been tolerant within the context of illiberal variation. Thus, there is little reason to believe that Canada has replicated either country of the Anglo-American world, notwithstanding the views of the two liberalistic schools of Canadian history. Theirs is a common error. The liberal and conservative liberal historians have regarded Canada as the ideological derivation of the liberalizing process which started long ago in western Europe and England and which arrived in the Thirteen Colonies-United States where local circumstance exaggerated it. But those same historians have failed to perceive that although Canadian ideological rhetoric has never been especially distinct from the Anglo-American, the roots of the *functional* ideology of Canada germinated and subsequently evolved in quite different circumstances. To ascertain those circumstances, one must examine pluralism.

Chapter Three:

Pluralism

I

Pluralism has been infinitely more complex than monolithic liberalism with its logically consistent value system. The major problem in examining the Canadian relationship to pluralism over the past three and a half centuries involves the fact that pluralism has varied in time and place. Contemporary pluralism in the United States, which has arisen as the Republic retreats from classical liberalism, cannot be expounded in the same fashion as Canadian or European pluralism might be expounded. The latter was a holdover from medieval feudalism, which appeared at the turn of this century to have been superseded, once and for all, by the alleged (liberalizing) nation states. But at present, the once predominant national and liberal age in Europe, like that in America, does not seem to be moving "forward" into a common Western ideological universality; quite the contrary, Europe appears to be retreating to more traditional values and perspectives, all of which has been rendered difficult to ascertain because of the imperatives of historical inquiry and the sheer immediacy of lingering liberal terminology.

That Canada has stood, in the conventional view, between the (North) American tradition and the European has made it especially difficult to identify the specifics of Canadian pluralism.

To facilitate the inquiry, this chapter will be arbitrarily divided: the first nine sections will examine the historical foundations of Canadian pluralism in terms of its feudal origins in Europe. The final sections will address the recent transformation of monolithic classical liberalism in the United States into contemporary corporate-liberalism and the general decline of liberal influence in the face of the revival of illiberal values in contemporary Europe.

II

In western Europe six centuries ago the exclusive values of each interest, estate, religious order, province, region, guild, city and so forth dictated the social reality: in short, highly localized and/or limited and/or exclusive values were of primary importance. Feudal society was characterized by ongoing, intense, often violent feuds between the various exclusive, localistic interests and the central government and also among the estates. From the ninth to the fifteenth century, the predominant socio-ideological interests varied from the highly localized predisposition of the nobility to the claim to universal authority by the Church, to the rise of the "national" (for want of a better term) monarchies — more or less in that chronological order. Eventually, in France after an attempted rejuvenation of the second estate had failed, the long suffering third estate came to the foreground in 1789 and its first significant political gesture was to destroy the legal and constitutional distinctions between the estates.

In standard historical thinking on the subject, there has been a tendency to conceive of power shifts between the estates from the ninth to the eighteenth century in terms of a "left-right" (liberal-illiberal) context. In fact, power shifts among the estates and the central government really had nothing whatsoever to do with a liberal (leftward) shift. The idea behind defining historical evolution in a left-right conceptual context rests on the degree of popularization of a particular set of individualistic values and the simultaneous elimination of traditional, limited, exclusive communitarian interests. Consequently, liberalization has been dictated not only by the degree to which ever more members of the populace adhere primarily to the same liberal value system, but also by the degree of erosion of exclusive, regional, provincial, estate and class loyalties.

In a society which is feudal or corporate and which experiences constantly shifting power among various exclusive interests, such power alterations by themselves bear no relation to liberalization. It is a point of speculation but one might well ask about the result deriving from a third estate victory in, say, the fourteenth century instead of the eighteenth, when Anglo-American concepts of liberalism were infecting French thought. Most probably, the fundamentals of the traditional order would not have been substantially upset, except that the burden of taxation might have become lighter for the third estate. But this, although significant to the process of social levelling, certainly does not mean that the general body of feudalistic law with its highly exclusive predisposition would have been swept away. After all, the notion of a popular society was still quite alien. In France the eventual victory of the third estate in 1789 did signal the collapse of the old order and did constitute a popular liberalizing gesture; this occurred when the leadership of the third estate (rather pretentiously) claimed to speak not for a limited interest — even if that estate was the vast majority — but for the entire French community.

Until the liberalizing and revolutionary acts of 1789 eliminated the most onerous obligations and privileges, not only was France a pluralistic society, but was so strongly a one as to be also corporate — by which is meant that the constituent parts of that pluralistic society had a legal and a constitutional basis for their existence. Not all pluralistic societies need have a corporate basis; it depends on the degree to which pluralism has evolved and the extent to which it has become an ingrained feature of a particular society. On the other hand, one would do well to remember that all societies exhibit a measure of pluralism and that no society, even a liberal one is totally homogeneous. The difference between pluralism and liberalism is one of degree.

In a liberal society the worth of the individual is generally of paramount significance, is legally enshrined, and is respected by the vast majority. In a pluralistic society each exclusive interest gives its allegiance to its limited community and devotes only its secondary allegiance to the larger community. Gradations exist, of course, between the two extremes. In light of Canada's rightward evolution, as expounded in the previous chapter, how can we determine the degree to which Canada has become a pluralistic society? That is to say, has Canada become corporate with legalized exclusive interests predominant, which is the most conservative manifestation of pluralism? Is Canada, for lack of a more precise term, simply pluralistic — highly diversified with exclusive groups giving their primary loyalty to special, limited or non-national interests, but such diversity, nonetheless, having no actual legal or constitutional foundation? Or is Canada a conservative liberal society; that is, one manifesting variously divisive tendencies among different groups, but nevertheless retaining a strong measure of sympathy for individualism?

III

It has been a traditional point of view that French Canada was a homogeneous society and that pluralism in Canada really originated with the British influence because the latter could not assimilate the former. The existence of two ethnic communities became the basis of a later and broader pluralism. Donald Creighton has traced the Canadian cultural mosaic to the multitude of identifiable groups who lived there in 1867 — the French, the English, the Irish, the Scotch. Once again, conditioned to some degree by the imperatives of the staples thesis, Creighton has argued that because Canada never rejected the old world, it retained the cultural distinctions of Britain which were strengthened by the French presence. When placed in transcontinental terms, prairie isolation aided cultural diversity. By way of reply to Creighton, one must remember that the *de facto* liberalism which was supplanting the earlier pluralistic ideology in Europe had received a conscious philosophical translation by John Locke in the seventeenth century which further weakened the old concept of entrenched and exclusive community interests. But the reverse seems to have happened in Canada: the British arrived with philosophical liberalism well developed only to have it erode rapidly under the functional reality of pluralism which the Conquest intensified. The staples trading system as an exclusive economic instrument had failed, by the very nature of its *raison d'être*, to engineer a popular market economy in the Canadas and to erect institutions conducive to the transmission and inculcation of liberal values in the Canadian masses. Nor did the masses ever manifest a single, integrating value system — irrespective of whether or not it was liberal — despite the centralized, paternalistic machinery of the staples system in their midst.

Late in the nineteenth century and early in the twentieth century — and then only very briefly, for some three decades — did the staples system in the guise of the wheat trade become far more popular (unlike the exclusiveness of fur, timber, and lumber before it) and introduce innumerable western farmers to the educating force of massive amounts of monetary capital. While containing liberalizing aspects, the trade in wheat was not of sufficient duration to re-educate society and, having largely extra-territorial associations, had no especially "Canadian" connotations which were necessary to achieve the ideological integration of that society. Indeed, under these circumstances, "things Canadian" conjured up a vision of old Canada West using its influence to assure itself of high tariffs which injured both the east and the west. Thus, even for that brief time when the staples system was capable of inculcating minimal liberal values, it was equally incapable of eroding provincial exclusivity.

David V J Bell[1] believes that the American Revolution played a major role in engineering the Canadian mosaic, appearing as it did at that instant when a mosaic type of society disappeared in the newly emergent United States. The United States, claims Bell, had a conscious monopoly of liberal-nationalism with a consequently strong sense of identity. The loyalists who were fundamentally liberal, continues Bell, arrived in Upper Canada but could not elevate their liberalism to nationalism because of the American connotations inherent in liberalism. In other words, in Bell's *schema* both whigs *and* tories shared the Lockeian (ie liberal) tradition. The necessity of being "un-American" confused the liberal tories of (English) Canada and, so Bell believes, this has produced the quest for the ever-elusive Canadian identity which, quite simply, is unrecognized liberalism. Then too, Bell has explained English Canada's decided "Britishness" in terms of its equation of liberalism with the United States, the conservative Canadian reaction to the United States having assumed a "British" translation. Of course, one may reply to Bell that ideologically (but not politically and constitutionally), there was nothing especially British about Canada and that, from an *ideological* perspective, anti-American gestures were also automatically anti-British ones. On the other hand, Bell readily admits that various benefits have derived from the Canadian mosaic: without such isolating features as a revolution and liberal-nationalism Canada has remained more willing to adapt to changing conditions than the United States. Where Bell may be fundamentally challenged, like Creighton, is in failing to question whether an increasingly pluralistic society is capable of being and/or remaining liberal.

There has been a third prevalent tendency which falls between the two liberalistic schools of Canadian history, a tendency to regard English Canada as having been guided by two examples, Great Britain and the United States, and to ignore the French Canadians with whom English Canadians have shared a constitution. In this perspective, English Canada has been characterized, relative to America, as accepting more limitation, exhibiting more deference to elitism, and having less optimism and faith in the future. The more conservative dimensions of English Canadian life have been traced to the British presence, which resulted in a counter-revolutionary tradition, monarchical institutions, a strong Anglican religious tradition, governmental authority to offset frontier influences, and the notion of a social mosaic. A point of dispute arises in the exaggeration of the Anglo-American tradition and in the further unwarranted assumption that two distinct ideological traditions can exist in the same state. By virtue of their association in the same political and constitutional framework, as shall be developed in due course, one tradition tends to predominate. The view that a conservative liberalism and illiberalism existed respectively in English Canada and French Canada has never been valid: the constitutional structure has provided a mechanism for the predominance of a common, non-popular, illiberal ideology from sea to sea.

IV

The St Lawrence community had long experienced the problem of what might be termed "competitive authority" — which stands in contrast to the concept of sovereign authority. The constitution of the *ancien regime* in France had involved three distinct groups — four, including the royal government, itself — each trying to adjust the socio-political situation to its own advantage. Neither the monarchy nor its competitors achieved a degree of power comparable to that of the English Parliament which, by virtue of its unlimited legislative authority, was more sovereign than any of the competing interests in France. The imported concept of pluralism in New France, originally based on derivative feudal ideas from the metropolis, was given a slight twist because of the absence of mature colonial estates. The competitive principle characterized the colonial leadership and the monarchy func- tioned toward that leadership as it did toward the estates in France. The constant referrals to Paris for final judgment in disputes among the Bishop, Intendant, and Governor over such matters as the brandy and fur trade, defence policies, Indian alliances, and various economic problems had assured the monarchy of a function in New France not dissimilar from that which it accom- plished in metropolitan France, the role of social mediator.

After the Conquest, the British governors in Quebec had started to function less as chief executive officers and more as local versions of the departed French monarchy. Although Donald Creighton sees the period until 1783 as one in which the seigneurial system and the British mercantile interests meshed in a succession to the French fur-trading empire, the colonial governors were clearly acting to defend the weaker conquered community against the pretensions of the stronger. The general antipathy of the governors toward commercial interests had developed against the background of mercantile rebelliousness in the Thirteen Colonies, the creation of the Court of Common Pleas in 1764 in which Roman Catholics could sit on juries and plead cases, the Quebec Act of 1774 which ended the earlier promise of representative institutions with an appointed legislative Council which became the bastion of the "French Party", and the refusal in

1778 of Governor Carleton to reveal instructions detrimental to the foregoing Party and its policy of paternalism. All the signs clearly suggest that executive power was being utilized to offset and restrain the mercantile interests.

Not until the half decade after the Revolutionary War did the state relax its seemingly anti-mercantile stance, conceding to the commercial interests unimpeded entry of American natural products into Canada and, in 1790, the Imperial preference for American products shipped to Britain by way of the St Lawrence. This established the basis for the commercial existence of Canada: free trade in the interior and a protected market in Britain. In addition, British legal practice was strengthened when ordinances were promulgated which provided for writs of *habeas corpus* and, somewhat later, for jury trials in civil cases. But to regard these gestures as part of a liberalizing process as Creighton does is to misread their ideological effect. Although the colonial governors and the authorities in London were undoubtedly guided by Imperial considerations in all these machinations, one must also remember that the habitant mentality, reared in a corporate climate, probably regarded the mercantile advances of the 1780s as the logical extension of the previous regime: one community "balanced off" against the other, with the agents of the state mediating, was the expected social reality. Nothing happened in the post-Conquest period to upset this situation; indeed, social reality was reinforcing traditional ideology.

It is a commonly held view that the Constitutional Act of 1791 was a further step in the process of liberalizing British America. Fernand Ouellet believes that the French Canadians used liberal institutions for conservative purposes, so that, in effect, only the form, not the substance was adopted. Helen Taft Manning regards the Constitution of 1791 as an attempt by the British government to avoid involvement in colonial politics by transferring broad and elastic powers to the colonial legislatures. By 1814 a curious reversal had developed within Lower Canada: the British Americans wished to undermine the constitution while the French Canadians wished to uphold and enjoy its benefits.[2] For Creighton, the Constitutional Act of 1791 was an indefensible gesture which isolated the vigorous Upper Canadian farmers from the equally vigorous and progressive Montreal business community and led the latter into a traditional late-feudal confrontation with a backward agricultural community. Eventually, the merchants and their ally, the state, emerged victorious in 1837 — or so Creighton claims. What has been ignored in this is the functional ideological impact of the 1791 Constitution on *all* Lower Canadian society. In fact, the constitutional readjustment imposed by Britain in 1791 simply opened the way to the re-establishment of the prevailing ideology within the newly structured context.

Lawrence A H Smith has put forth the thesis[3] that French Canadian leaders in the Assembly had consciously sought out British constitutional examples and precedents as a basis for solving their provincial problems. In that sense, French Canadian leaders were not radicals but British-styled constitutionalists who were seeking to check the existing power structure. Freedom involved an attempt to balance power within the state structure. What Smith fails to grasp is that, despite British parliamentary divisions, British society was being popularly united by liberal values, whereas Lower Canada, by virtue of greater (illiberal) pluralism, was not similarly united since exclusive ethnic-economic values predominated over any others. Lower Canadian constitutional divisions began to coincide with social ones to a degree that was not possible in Britain. In a functional sense, the socio-political reality was not that of post-sixteenth century liberalizing Britain but was much more that of pre-revolutionary France with its distinct, non-integrating interests. What has been especially difficult for the historian has involved perception of the functional reality of Lower Canada, when elsewhere in the Western world the popular trend was toward the liberal left. Lower Canadian society, despite the acquisition of superficial British institutions against a background of Anglo-American rhetoric, was moving in the opposite direction.

Having received the form of British institutions, Lower Canada lacked indigenous liberalizing substance. Competing interests continued to exhaust themselves in constant confrontation; the French Canadian agrarian majority in the elected Assembly opposed the Executive and Legislative Councils appointed for their political reliability. It is inconceivable that this "divide and conquer" approach was ever an articulated Imperial intention, but, in fact, it did insure what London most wanted, maintenance of the colonial *status quo*. Neither interest, it must be remembered, was totally trustworthy from the Imperial point of view. The French and, especially, the American Revolutions had indicated the violent potential of unchecked colonial mercantile proclivities which invited Imperial suspicion of the linguistically English commercial interests. On the other hand, the historical and inherent linguistic associations of the habitant made him suspect, almost by definition, to British sensitivities.

The Imperial authority which operated through its appointed governors remained aloof and attracted as little attention as possible. An Imperial dispatch to the Governor, Sir James Craig, in September 1810 pointed out that even if the Constitutional Act of 1791 was not functioning according to expectation, there was no provision for intervention by the Imperial Parliament.[4] If an appointee — and Craig is the prime example — was over-zealous and ultimately detrimental to the Imperial position through favouring one of the local interests, he was checked — in Craig's case by recall. In 1827, Lord Dalhousie vetoed the election of L J Papineau as Speaker of the Assembly, which contributed to political instability: Dalhousie was subsequently censured by London. Similarly, the Imperial authorities had always refused the Assembly control of patronage. Such a concession would have constituted an excessive power shift to the former and removed from the Imperial authority, through its connection with the colonial executive, the ultimate weapon (short of violence) in achieving a measure of social control.

Perhaps the institutionalization of the power balance may be best illustrated by the Imperial concession of 1831. London simply surrendered control of revenue to the Lower Canadian House of Assembly without a civil list, so that if the traditional sources of revenue were insufficient, the payment of civil servants had to be voted by the lower house. Subsequently, the executive branch was checked by the legislative branch. Since the evolution of the English constitution had been based almost exclusively on repeated struggles over finance between the executive and legislative branches, one could argue that the Imperial concession to Lower Canada amounted to a liberalization gesture by opening the prospect for a comparable development in that province. But there was, of course, one significant difference: the struggle between the English crown and its parliament was self-contained with no external recourse (if one neglects the papacy in the late medieval period), whereas, in Lower Canada, the distant Imperial authority never surrendered its ultimate regulatory power so that the genuine English process of liberalization was never part of the Lower Canadian experience. The classic example involves the deadlock which developed between the executive and legislative branches in 1833. Since this crisis was not amenable to a local solution over the next several years, Lord John Russell, on behalf of the Imperial authority, issued his Ten Resolutions in 1837 which restored functional colonial government by applying a countervailing force against the agrarian majority in the House of Assembly and strengthening the colonial executive: Russell permitted the latter to spend revenue without legislative consent. The traditional concept of the state acting as *deus ex machina* was as functional in 1837 as it had been under the French authority and continued to reinforce the traditional ideology.

The outcome of the Rebellion of 1837 was just another manifestation of the rightward tendency toward social corporatism and governmental mediation. That Rebellion, of course, had threatened both the mercantile interests and the primacy of the state by attempting to shift power completely into the grasp of those claiming to speak for the French Canadians. This was a blatant denial of the ingrained fashion in which the habitant himself had grown to expect the state and the countervailing mercantile interests to operate. The attempted leftward shift and all that it entailed — the concept of the supremacy of individual rights over the concept of community interests and the weakening of the state — were antithetical to the habitant mentality. Irrespective of the degree of sympathy based on language and custom which the revolutionaries had engendered, the vast majority of the habitants stood aside while the state did exactly what was expected of it — it reasserted internally (just as it had done in 1775 and in 1812 against external threats) its predominant position as the supreme arbiter of public affairs in Lower Canada.

It seems evident that the Rebellion of 1837 was not a Creightonian commercial-agrarian conflict with the former interests emerging victorious over the latter; the conflict involved the successful expansion of an ancient social order which the British presence was inadvertently encouraging. Although the commercial interests were on the winning side, it was emphatically not their victory. The state alone had triumphed. Not the local commercial state with its empire along the St Lawrence, as Creighton would say, but rather the state in its most terrible and potentially irresponsible form, the state as *deus ex machina*. If the state and the mercantile interests appeared to be in league, then the latter and many historians since have rather badly misread the relationship between these interests and the state. The state was not fundamentally hostile to the habitants; the state was not fundamentally favourable to the merchants, although it was pragmatically so in 1837. The state played no favourites; it was above all that.

More than a decade later, the events surrounding the achievement of responsible government were the logical result of the prevailing extraterritorial constitutional structure and of the Canadian ideology. Governmental policy in 1849 continued to reflect pragmatic alterations in Imperial emphasis. As in 1837, the government was not overtly hostile to the injured group — in this instance, the mercantile interests — but was only incidentally so. Instead of a liberal victory, the achievement of responsible government was associated with illiberal French Canadian interests who used their newly found political indispensability to block any essential liberal reform. In alliance with linguistically English groups external to Lower Canada-Quebec over the following half century, the Bleus effectively influenced the ideological evolution of the transcontinental Canadian state. Consequently, responsible government assured continuing social diversity by elevating predominantly limited community interests — which in a Canadian context meant an exclusive, divisive ethnicity — over such popular integrating liberal principles as individual merit and freedom.

V

In a refinement of the staples thesis, a Marxist observer, Tom Naylor[5], has distinguished merchant capital from capital in other forms, and from the classes necessarily associated with those forms. Naylor claims that the shattering of Canada may be traced to growing economic contradictions; merchant capital has generally been non-adventurous, low-risk. It has encouraged a centralist state structure to protect its interests in the extractive mechanisms of the staples system and its more mature expressions — banking, finance, utilities, transportation. Dependent by nature, the merchant capitalists had sought advantages from the extraterritorial metropolis, Great Britain, and, more recently, the United States. Translated into politics, a conservative constitutional structure (as opposed to a liberal one) was the logical counterpart of predominant merchant capital with its desire for state imposed regulation. Only in the late 1870s did merchant capital interests encourage institution of a "National Policy" of industrialization to build the population. Foreign industrial capital was attracted to create a series of branch plants in Canada but, insists Naylor, the Policy certainly did not protect the existing but weak Canadian industrial base. Instead, the Canadian merchant capitalists benefited from increased economic activity in their traditional areas of dominance by servicing (American) direct investment in industry. As, moreover, banking, finance, communications, and utilities which had been built by British debt investment responded to economic stimulus, branch plant expansion provided needed capital to retire the British debt, thereby helping to cut the old staples links with Britain.

One of Naylor's essential points is to attribute the constitutional climate to the rendering of merchant capital, the predominant interest, through its extraterritorial associations. Naylor claims, by reason of his Marxist assumption of the necessary association of capital type, class, and ideology, that the economically predominant class has dictated the nature of Canada. But Canada has been a land with an extraordinarily powerful pluralistic and/or feudalistic legacy, a pluralism which in medieval Europe was also characterized by the issues of centralism versus regionalism/provincialism, and territorialism (loyalty to the local king or prince) versus extraterritorialism (loyalty to the papacy). Nothing in the merchant capital tradition as expounded by Naylor was at variance with the pluralistic tradition. The various political and constitutional experiments through which Canada passed and which resulted in the structure of 1867 represented the adjustments of a constant ideology to the fluidity of "modernizing" imperatives. What prevailed was not the economically induced ideology of the predominant class as Marxist theory dictates but was rather the imperative of subordinated Bleu interests whose essential ideology has survived until this day. Because Canada was defined to the right of economically based monolithic liberalism, merchant capital easily transmuted into new fields of endeavour which were not truly at variance with the Canadian ideology. In pluralistic Canada, no single interest, economic or otherwise, has ever *totally* dominated the state without regard to countervailing forces. Marxists, because of their particular ideological screen, have been most neglectful of the prevalent ideology of the *apparently* subordinate Bleu interest and of the political economy of 1867 that accorded with it.

Innis and Naylor, who regard Confederation as a search for new markets, tend to see Confederation as an imposed situation, largely divorced from indigenous ideological imperatives. Although Donald Creighton has also relied heavily on the staples theory, his perception of Confederation has given greater weight to domestic influences. Creighton stressed the essentially political nature of Confederation, claiming that the Fathers of the "new nationality" wanted to continue a tradition that was at once both British and British American. Reference to the writing of John Conway will aid in illustrating a basic dilemma in analysing the ideology of Confederation Canada. On one hand, Conway brilliantly explains the fundamental differences between the United States and Canada, proving, by his own evidence, the very illiberality of the latter; on the other hand, Conway inexplicably accepts Professor Edward McWhinney's view of the British North America Act as a liberal document.[6] Surely this is logically inconsistent: if Canada has been similar to the United States, then

Canada has been liberal; if Canada has not been similar, then Canada has not been liberal. How could a land exhibiting strong extraterritorialism, a relativistic and non-messianic sense of political democracy, and substantial pluralism possibly be classed as liberal? Basic to this difficulty is the tendency to regard Canada as "British", a tendency which fails to distinguish between politics and ideology: for while Canada did have British constitutional and economic connections, Canada has never been *ideologically* British.

Suffering from a similar blindness with different results are Michel Brunet and Alfred Dubuc who have allowed for the French Canadian role but have misread and downplayed its significance. Arguing from a preconceived and unjustified association of class with ideology, Dubuc[7] claims that the 1837 Rebellions had removed the lower middle class and thereby encouraged a capitalist and bourgeois state structure which was eventually reflected in the Act of Union of 1840 and the Confederation of 1867. Both of the latter, contends Dubuc, were nothing more than gestures of public finance by the dominant clique and, consequently, reflected their liberal ideas on political economy. The difficulty with this approach is Dubuc's failure to recognize the fundamental reversal of evolution in Canada, which tends to invalidate his Marxist assumptions. The ideology which was enshrined in constitutional law in 1867 came no more from the capitalists above than from those below, no more from the English speakers than from the French Canadians.

With a position not dissimilar from Dubuc's in his assessment of French Canadian subordination, Michel Brunet[8] has regarded the vast panorama of Canadian history as a series of setbacks for the French Canadians at the hands of the English-speaking Canadians. The latter had failed to accept the former as partners — or, at least, such is Brunet's claim. It is only partly correct. Only in the areas of objectively sensible values such as language and (possibly) religion did the French Canadians ever receive setbacks under Confederation — in New Brunswick in 1871, in Manitoba in 1896 and again more decisively in 1916, in the controversy surrounding the Autonomy Bills of 1905, and in Regulation 17 of the Ontario Department of Education in 1913. But all of the fore-

going involved only objective political defeats; at the more fundamental ideological level, French Canadian illiberal conservatism
had won out in the Confederation of 1867. Paradoxically, in fact,
French Canadian ideological success in 1867 opened the way for
subsequent political disasters. What could have saved the linguistically French from an "English" political counterstroke after
1867 would have involved enshrining in constitutional law, when
the opportunity presented itself in 1867, certain "inalienable" and
"self evident" principles such as the sanctity of different cultures,
languages and religions. But that would have been a gesture too
blatantly illiberal in fostering the legal creation of autonomous
estates for the Imperial government which had to legislate the
Canadian constitution.

On the other hand, the parameters within which the British
North America Act was framed by virtue of the Seventy Two
Resolutions were certainly not liberal, lacking as they did, stress
on private property and civil rights. The British North America
Act did not precisely articulate either liberal or illiberal principles,
either individualism or community interests, although the latter
did tend to predominate. Because the constitution was nebulous, it
did not inhibit the reassertive ideology of French Canada and the
Bleus with their unswerving stress on limited (ethnic) community
interests. Unfortunately, when community interests were associated with ethnicity and then became intermeshed with politics,
voting power became a prime consideration in a country with
representative institutions. The relative shift in voting power from
the "French" to the "English" late in the nineteenth century
caused the former to be excluded from a transcontinental political
role. Thus, the French Canadian stress on community interests
precluded a clearly liberal constitution and, paradoxically,
politically injured their community's ethnic status outside
Quebec. The Bleu ideological victory of illiberal pluralism led
directly to the Bleu political defeat in transcontinental terms. Nor
did the Liberal Party's eventual electoral victory in 1896
downgrade illiberal pluralism as the functional ideology of
Canada.

Liberalism had come to support the staples system as is shown
by its commitment to the continued construction of extractive

transportation mechanisms, the railways. Although Liberalism began to approximate the Conservative Party's earlier National Policy after 1896, it did not displace Conservativism as the unqualified high tariff party, even if Liberalism did flirt with the preferential tariff after the 1896 election. Ultimately, the Liberal Party retained its decidedly lower tariff proclivities, a position which was less able to defend the east-west trade axis so basic to Confederation Canada and was, consequently, somewhat less "Canadian" than Conservativism. This led to the great paradox of 1911 — that Conservativism was politically less "Canadian" with its British extraterritorialism but more "Canadian" economically; Liberalism was just the opposite, politically supportive of a Canadian Navy but trapped, economically, by the dual non-Canadianism of the regional-continentalism of reciprocity. Politically, Prime Minister Sir Wilfrid Laurier had assumed a position, in terms of the socio-ideological spectrum, somewhat more leftward than the two rightward tending ethnic groups: this was a Canadian position, analogous to that of the old Conservative Party before it fragmented. But the Liberals, too, were subsequently forced rightward. First came the Boer War which eroded the localistic Canadian emphasis in politics and which encouraged a reviving empathy for extraterritorialism dormant in English Canada since the late 1840s. Second was the rightward ethnic proclivity, with no overriding, single, especially Canadian focal point.

That the First World War shattered the empires of central and eastern Europe by bringing into sharp relief the forces of ethnic nationalism is part of conventional wisdom. In Canada, which was far from active military operations, the process of ethnic animosity never achieved its logical conclusion. But in Canada, too, the political instruments of unity — the political parties — definitely ceased to operate in a unifying "national" fashion. The Conservatives had lost French-speaking Quebec in 1917 over the conscription issue. For the Liberals the situation was somewhat different. The electoral result in 1911 in Quebec had indicated already that the Liberal Party was in danger of following the long-declining Conservatives to political oblivion in Quebec. Thus, when the conscription crisis occurred, Laurier astutely refused to engage in any gestures hostile to the French speaking interests of Quebec. But in displacing the hitherto growing *nationaliste* appeal, the Laurier Liberals paradoxically committed their Party to a strong, potentially non-Canadian position in the sense that the Party was associating itself with an exclusive, quite limited interest. The old Bleu imperative, exclusive and localistic, had found in 1896 and retained in 1917 a new instrument to limit federal initiatives. As in central Europe the shattering process was undermining Canada, although, of course, it was less evolved — if only because the renewed intensity of the east-west staples system during wartime helped counteract the country's potential political fragmentation.

VI

Most Marxist commentators pay especial attention to the linkages between the state and class inequality, but this chapter has aimed at showing that the Canadian state has never been *fundamentally* associated with any particular class, ethnic group or, in fact, any limited interest. Although the emphasis of various Marxist authors has differed, they have generally claimed that the evolution of the Canadian state has been a direct by-product of its capitalistic circumstance and that the state created conditions based on public policy to benefit the bourgeois class in its accumulation of private wealth. What must be stressed, by way of reply, is that Canada has never been a capitalistic state in the Marxist sense of the term, where, *de facto*, capitalism has been associated with the oppressive excesses of (classical) liberalism. Consequently, Canada cannot be judged in terms of necessary class tension based on economic inequality with the predominant class supported implicitly by the state.

The recent past may have found the state on the side of interests both capitalistic and "Anglo" but this condition — even if correct — has not been a *fundamental* condition of the Canadian state. Pronounced class distinctions are simply another aspect of a society primarily distinguished by the divisions of an ethnic, religious, provincial and/or regional nature. As an extension of the foregoing, one might note that the state in Canada has exhibited little unity of intent, for, in accordance with the prevailing ideology, the state itself has always been fragmented. Nor has this simply been a consequence of the vast geography to be governed, a pragmatic response to legitimate regional concerns — although, it must be conceded, geography has contributed its share. The fragmentation of the state in Canada has been basic to the functional and preliberal ideology. For this reason, Canadians have often given their primary allegiance to the provinces and/or the regions, rather than to the central authority.

It has long been part of the conventional wisdom of the conservative liberal school that the trans-Atlantic trade in staples and the British and/or European connection had been essential to the well-being of Confederation, and that the collapse of the east-west trade in staples opened the way to undue American influence. More recently, Tom Naylor has expanded this view to embrace a class perspective, namely, that the alleged "ruling class" in Canada has become superfluous to management of the continental system in the north. This alleged ruling class had arisen, of course, from the debris of its predecessor, the merchant capitalists, who had overdeveloped the Canadian economy insofar as it related to the east-west staples trade to the neglect of a truly Canadian industrialization programme. Although the "ruling class" with its interests in banking, finance, communications and utilities is regarded as the strongest independent Canadian interest, it is, when compared to the regional-continental interests centred in the provinces, relatively weak. From this has followed, claims Naylor, the political eclipse of Ottawa relative to the provinces and the general recolonization of Canada relative to the United States. But working along the same lines, one could also argue that the irrelevance of the "ruling class' and, more especially, the federal power structure through which it functions, began, not with the Americanization of the capitalistic economy, but rather with the irrelevance of Ottawa to British Imperial objectives in the late nineteenth century. Working through the Judicial Committee of the British Privy Council, the Imperial attack on centralized authority in Canada coincided, more or less, with the completion of the internal transportation system, Ottawa losing its necessity, one can only assume, after the Canadian Pacific Railway was constructed. The attack on the "ruling class" and its visible instrument, the federal government, long pre-dated the American intrusion, the decline of the east-west trade in staples, and the recolonization of Canada which both conservative liberals and Marxists decry.

While it had been advantageous to create a powerful government in Ottawa in 1867 to defend Imperial interests in North America, that same authority had become an obstacle to new Imperial initiatives in the late nineteenth and early twentieth centuries. Ottawa did not blindly follow Imperial desires, especially in regard to manpower requirements for imperialistic escapades; nor did Prime Minister Sir Wilfrid Laurier accept the ambitious plan for an Imperial Federation. In its various decentralizing decisions the Judicial Committee was, to some degree, removing the obstacle posed by Ottawa. Had war not arrived in 1914 and with it the necessity of organizing the continental interior under strong leadership once again, it is not absolutely improbable that, ultimately, direct political links between London and the provinces may have been re-established. As it was, the post-war state in Canada was left badly fragmented. Of course, Marxist historians would simply reply that such fragmentation has served best the accumulating objectives of significant groups within the predominant class. It may be incidentally correct that specific interests have been profiting from a weak central authority and rampant provincialism, but equally evident is the fact that various longstanding non-economic factors with no especial class-accumulation connotation have contributed significantly to the fragmenting state structure in Canada.

VII

According to Wallace Clement[9] who has absorbed much of Tom Naylor's historical perspective, Canadian society has been characterized by an exclusive corporate elite which, through its economic and media involvement, has been the predominant factor in Canadian society. The corporate elite, claims Clement in contradistinction to Naylor's position, remains vital and maintains its dominance through interlocking associations, private and/or exclusive clubs, private schools, directorships in large corporate and/or media organizations which, in turn, promote an "orthodox" vision of the world designed to lull the masses into acquiescence. Basically, the liberal democratic nation state, claims Clement, who regards Canada as liberal, democratic, and national, has been at variance with the reality of Canadian politics and society. That society has been highly structured, not especially conducive to vertical mobility, and designed to render profit to private interests by the use of public funds and support. Clement also regards the corporate elite as a by-product of commerce, but with the merchant elite in its present metamorphosis having retained vigour by servicing the American penetration of manu-facturing and resource development. In that Clement perceives the Canadian elite as drawing its strength from continentalism rather than being immediately menaced by it, he denies Naylor's conclusion. But, like Naylor, Clement agrees that a "national" Canadian bourgeoisie, by which he means an industrial one with distinctly Canadian loyalties, has not arisen.

What is most baffling are Clement's obvious sociological insights and observations which run counter to his assumptions, insofar as these relate to Canada as a nation state and liberal democracy. The elitist structure which he describes in detail does not conform to popular nationality or liberalism. In this, Clement represents an example of the imposed rhetoric of the progressivist liberal or (pseudo-)Marxist historical perspective denying what is empirically evident. Clement really describes a neo-feudal and/or corporate tendency and appears to be oblivious to its significance. The very use of historical perspective he borrows from Naylor and the staples theorists and, ultimately, Western historical theory, makes no provision for non-progressive concepts of history. The notion of an illiberal Canada within the context of the West simply does not exist. Clement has misunderstood the Canadian context through the inadvertent misappropriation of historical inquiry and, consequently, his admonition that Canada has not realized its promise as a land of opportunity is improper. Feudal societies make no such promises: liberal ones do. And on that turns a cruel bit of irony.

Clement derides liberalism, the one ideology which holds out a measure of hope for social justice. His claim that liberal democracies have not attempted to achieve equality of condition is a non-issue: first, with reference to Canada, one may indicate that, while democratic, Canada has never been truly liberal. Secondly, Western liberalizing societies exclusive of Canada were definitionally anti-feudal, an imperative for political and legal equality in an eventual democratic guise and one engendering vertical mobility in the socio-economic realm. Lastly, truly (classical) liberal societies had few highly sophisticated structures; even government was simply organized. The recent departure from classical liberalism was partly caused by industrial and business corporatism, which instituted structural or organizational neo-feudalism but which retained the liberal economic ideal, the *laissez faire* philosophy. Egalitarianism and brotherhood were thereby limited to politics and law.

Into this contradictory divorcement of liberal constitutional-politics on one hand and free-market economics with its inbuilt adversities for many individuals on the other, flowed the socialistic philosophies of the nineteenth century. The new business and industrial corporate reality arose under the retained theory of *laissez faire* which had been more appropriate to simpler times. The far left of the socio-ideological spectrum is supposed by socialists to be monolithic, based on universal notions of a justice, essentially social and economic, the achievement of which renders politics unnecessary. The divorcement of structured industrial economics and fluid egalitarian politics in the post-classical liberal period shattered the tendency toward monolithism in a functional sense and impelled a socio-ideological regression. Like liberals, Marxists and socialists, given their progressivist mind-set, seem unable to discern regressive (neo-feudal) reality. Hence, the inherent functional dilemma in Clement's call for justice (ie equality of condition) in Canada. To alter substantially the existing concentration of economic and political power, a country would have to follow, in general terms, the liberalization process so characteristic of the Anglo-Americans. If anything, the two major processes which Clement identifies since 1951 tend to confirm that illiberalism is deepening; the long-standing centralization of economic power is continuing unabated and so is American penetration into manufacturing and the resource sector.

Clement's sociological observations about the existence and activities of the corporate elite probably are correct. That is not in dispute. What is being disputed is the nature of the Canadian ideology. It was, Naylor and Clement would say, defined by the presence of staples-based merchant capital restricting Canadian industrial capital, whereas the contention here bases ideological derivation in Canada upon a force of circumstance largely external to economics. If the staples system was founded, economically, on merchant and finance capital, then it was only so organized because these types of capital did not collide with the prevailing illiberal thrust.

VIII

Douglas Hartle, in a presentation to the Canadian Tax Foundation,[10] discerned a "new feudalism" emerging in Canadian society by virtue of its increasing stratification. One may well reply to Hartle that this "feudalism" is not "new", the necessary pluralism and exclusiveness on which it rests having long been present. Anticipating Hartle's comments, Wallace Clement has identified obstacles involving vertical mobility. According to Clement, three deeply entrenched elites are responsible for this situation: an indigenous one dominating finance, utilities and transportation; a comprador one of senior management controlling the branch plants; a parasite one, extraterritorial in nature, controlling the multinational corporations. Combining the points of view of Clement and Hartle, one cannot but help seeing certain Canadian parallels to traditional west European feudalism. What has made the feudal elite of old and the present elite in Canada similar to each other and quite different from the elitism of liberal societies is that the former rests on stratified privileges, and remains largely exclusive and isolated, whereas the latter rests on merit associated with fluid financial reward. In Canada, the old staples business class has become an exclusive and entrenched interest. Capitalism in Canada married a feudalistic ideology of totally exclusive interests, an ideology quite different and distinct from liberalism with its careers open to talent. The Marxist belief that Canada may be examined by a conventional Marxist approach because Canada has been a replica of the Anglo-American world is dead wrong. And yet, one cannot be totally unsympathetic toward the Marxist vision in light of the Canadian reality: just as the old European nobility lost its military necessity with the popularization of warfare and the Church its appeal to powers of salvation in a secular age, so have the entrenched elites of Canada which organized the continental interior lost their *raison d'être*, the principle of "peace, order and good government" having been long ago established as the basis of the present Confederation.

IX

There is another, often unrecognized aspect to the problem of Canadian pluralism which involves a much more profound and empirically less evident type of diversity. Both liberal schools of Canadian history have made the (liberal) assumption that the empirical method is fundamentally sound in its application to all aspects of historical inquiry. This rests on the further assumption that economics, politics, and objective social reality are all aspects of a coherent, logically consistent ideology. In Marxist thought, too, derived as it largely has been from criticism of liberal(izing) societies, economic circumstance is believed to dictate homogeneity both in the objective and subjective realms. But Canadian pluralism has resulted in a discrepancy between conscious belief and subconscious function, between appearance and functional ideology. In large measure, this discrepancy derives from the fact that Canada has been a "recipient" society *vis-à-vis* the Anglo-American world and Western Civilization, rather than an indigenously creative one. The receptive function has involved alien linguistic concepts which have been injudiciously adapted to a contrary historical evolution (ie contrary to liberalism). This is why Canadians can consciously utilize various liberal concepts, use parliamentary methods, and practice an apparently British type of democracy, while the Canadian ideology is illiberal.

A liberal society represents a cohesiveness which binds concepts and empirical reality, the one an extension of the other. In Canada where the ideology evolved contrary to the liberal Anglo-American, historical "reality" has been even more difficult to distinguish than in a liberal situation, because not only was pluralism socially divisive, it was ideologically so, in the sense that concepts associated with it were divided from, or set apart from, or not representative of, the social reality. The concepts being used have often been imports which have not coincided with Canadian circumstance and hence have been an inadequate mechanism for ideological comprehension; for example, the achievement of responsible government and parliamentary institutions in Canada have not necessarily been indicative of liberalism, although such has often been interpreted as a "British" liberalization gesture. The empirical method in Canadian history has generally been less effective than in liberal societies; its conceptual tools have not been indigenous and, consequently, have not been logically consistent extensions of the society which they are being used to investigate. A real hiatus has existed between the historian with his alien concepts and the object of his investigation, the Canadian historical circumstance. This irrationality has arisen out of the meshing of a (residual feudalistic) pluralism with a highly exclusive staples system, neither of which fundamentally threatened the other. Traditional concepts of empirical test do not seem to take proper cognizance of such non-integrated structures as the Canadian. In Anglo-American society, a "sameness" of thought conceptualization and objective reality makes observation, comprehension, and conclusions relatively easy to reach. A too insensitive application of empirical assumptions — all quite valid in a liberal society — have tended toward confusion in Canada.

The liberal and conservative liberal schools have been, conceptually, in terms of their frames of reference, both manifestations of traditional illiberal Canadianism. Both schools have tended to place Canada in a dependent position *vis-à-vis* an extraterritorial power structure and both have falsely assumed the fundamental integration of Canadian society — economically, politically, *and* ideologically. For this reason, neither school has taken proper cognizance of the discrepancy between political economy on one hand and ideology on the other. As victims themselves of the fundamental irrationality of the old order, both liberal schools had a quite false perception of the basic nature of Canada and neither school was consequently able to provide solutions. Locked into the traditional irrational structure, these schools have devoted far too much effort to mutual recrimination, since there is little value in labelling "British" or "American". Canada is neither, and both schools have failed to recognize that fact.

The rhetoric of liberalism in Canada has been a filter, blinding innumerable commentators irrespective of their persuasions — Marxist, socialist, conservative, liberal. Critics have assumed that the rhetorical expression by individuals of their alleged ideologies is a valid measure of ascertaining the ideological mix of Canada. Such is not so, because in pluralistic Canada the conceptual framework bears no *necessary* reference to socio-ideological reality. In the Anglo-American world (or in any society where ideology and social reality are fairly homogeneous), the connection between thought and action, and also between rhetoric and reality, has probably been very close. But in Canada, because of its exclusive community emphasis and the disintegrating quality of its socio-ideological system, the connection between concepts and functional reality has been weak and nebulous. This is why Canada may be rhetorically liberal, and not so, functionally. In short, the methodology of inquiry into socio-ideological systems appropriate to the Anglo-American world, which has been highly integrated, cannot be adapted to Canada.

X

Pluralism, in its varied manifestations, is again rejuvenating itself in traditional areas of influence, a situation which commentators committed to the liberal/Marxist vision of a progressive, necessarily liberal/Marxist future have failed to comprehend. Understanding this development has not been rendered easier by the traditional and ingrained liberal/Marxist tendency to denigrate feudalism and to regard the very concept as a hold-over from the distant past. True, the guise of the medieval corporate flowering as feudalism has passed away, but its ideological legacy has been most insidious. It has not expired but has survived the "national" period (about which much more will be said in the following chapter), and, in the contemporary period, shows more vitality than classical liberalism. If anything, the Western world appears to be heading again into feudalism or, at least, some associated corporate, communitarian form. Precisely because its present rendering is a traditional socio-ideological reassertion in a new guise, often decked out in liberal terminology, the empirical method is not especially relevant to an investigation of its values.

In the last century, the borderlands of the West were established by the transcontinental United States at the Mexican and Canadian borders and by revolutionary France in Europe. In this century, the frontier has been retreating. The pronounced exclusivity of ethnicity or, perhaps more properly, ethnic nationalism, which shattered the lingering medieval Hapsburg and Ottoman systems, has often been regarded as an expression of a new awareness in the nineteenth and twentieth centuries — a gesture toward modernity. Such a perspective is deceptive. Ethnic nationalism was essentially a throwback to, and a reaffirmation of, a medieval sense of exclusivity and limitation, until recently distinguished by "race", language, culture, and, on occasion, religion and class. Only the terminology of the phenomenon was new: because the medieval imperial structures passed away in the first two decades of this century amidst the rhetoric of Wilsonian liberalism and left in their wake (exclusive, parochial, ethnic) nation states, it has been easy to forget that these states represented a feudal afterglow. The destruction of their inefficient precursors, the Ottomans and the Hapsburgs, did not necessarily constitute a great progressive gesture because the destruction of the old order did not direct the successor states into the age of popular liberal progress.

True, the successor states utilized the rhetoric of Anglo-American liberalism but, from the point of view of functional ideology, corporatism shortly revived in the Fascist and Nazi guise throughout central Europe. The symbols of medieval feudalism —

serfdom and the most obvious manifestations of exclusive class power and privilege — had, of course, passed away in the Hapsburg Empire in the mid-nineteenth century. Moreover, despite the rise of self-centered ethnicity, most of the successor states, paradoxically perhaps, retained a certain deference to extra-territorial authority which was a by-product of their immediately subordinate past and of the feudal system which had preceded it. *Realpolitik* played an undeniable subordinating role too, especially after Hitler revived Germany, as did Stalin, Russia. In the absence of traditional protectors in Vienna and Istanbul, Moscow and Berlin became beneficiaries of central European deference. What must be borne in mind is that liberal theory asserts the necessary emancipation of Man, both as an atomistic individual and as a nation. Because central Europe had no indigenous tradition of genuine liberalism and its imported liberal rhetoric was not sufficient for the task, the area reverted to its traditional, deferential socio-ideological stance before the newly emergent imperial powers.

Even the Anglo-American progenitor of liberalism is retreating. Great Britain has been coming to an increasing appreciation of its pre-liberal tradition. Nineteenth century liberalism has collapsed before the victorious axis of resurgent ethnicity in Ireland, Scotland, and Wales and of socialism, which two, by virtue of their communitarian tendencies, have been natural (anti-liberal) allies. The British state in this century has been manifesting itself, not so much as the traditional defender of rights in property but rather as the regulator of social and economic justice. Classical liberalism had counselled individual prudence and discretion based on participation in government by necessarily rational property owners; democracy has appropriated the political institutions erected by liberalism and so broadened access that the elimination of liberalism permitted the tyranny (from a liberal viewpoint) of singular interests which may be described, more properly, as a type of neo-feudal estatism.

British democracy, unlike the American variety, did not arrive hand in hand with liberalism but was only achieved after the liberal period had commenced decline. Democracy arrived in Britain as an aspect, not only of political democracy as in the United States, but also as an aspect of social democracy. And social democracy was not democratic in the purely liberal sense, but was rather the instrument of special interests that had not regarded themselves as the beneficiaries of the liberal period. Their limited "class" perspectives represented a throwback to the pre-liberal past. The retention of feudal forces, royalty, lords, commons, the church — anglicized, not Roman — automatically preserved the seeds of medieval feudalism and thereby prevented the victory of a totally monolithic liberalism in Britain as in America. Indeed, under the liberalizing camouflage of 1689, feudalism was transmuted and gained a new lease on life as the aristocracy was rendered more secure and the House of Commons became more exclusive as the payment of members was terminated. At its inception, English liberalism had been less egalitarian than American liberalism in 1776.

Unlike the United States where a political power shift within a monolithic system of liberalism has never represented fundamental change in the system, political adjustments in post-liberal Britain have represented, *de facto,* a feudal revival. In rejecting individualism, a new communitarianism has automatically flowered. In medieval times, only the first two estates had seriously struggled with the monarchy for authority: the third estate was never a serious contender. But in post-liberal Britain with the power of the masses having been established by democracy, on a numerical basis alone the "third estate" won out. Like any feudal class the "third estate" has not used its power physically to destroy other interests: ideologically it could not, because the object is domination, not destruction, just as it was seven hundred years ago when, variously, the church, nobles, and monarch were predominant.

XI

By fully embracing liberalism — the ideology of universality, revolution, technological change, and "modernity" — the United States had, so to speak, detached itself from the socio-ideological spectrum of the old world. While Great Britain retains a decided and resurgent tory strain, the United States has not, strictly speaking, regressed, but has moved towards a new, unique type of structure — corporate-liberalism. American corporate-liberalism must not be confused with the resurgent (neo-)feudal strain of Great Britain and Europe: this may be better understood by reference to the functional definitions of conservativism in Europe/Canada and in the United States. Conservativism in Europe/Canada has been the "right" and in the United States the "left", because conservativism has denoted the ideological point of origin. Europe, and, by logical extension, Canada, evolved from feudalism, which had come to full maturity about 1000 A.D. Liberalism constituted the socio-ideological departure point in the United States as represented by the Articles of Confederation. The federalist reaction of the late 1780s *somewhat* "de-individualized" American society. Federalism opened the way to a more centralized and invigorated government; economically, the first national bank also initiated a rightward drift. None of this means that the United States has been reabsorbing feudalism or "toryism" or other aspects of the European tradition. These had been eliminated, as subsequent Federalist failures at a more pronounced tory reassertion indicated. Consequently, as contemporary America moves away from monolithic liberal homogeneity, America moves alone along a corporate-liberal path unique in global history.

Because the original points of departure defined "conservativism" in the respective ideological journeys both of Europe/Canada and of the United States, it logically follows that their associated concepts of liberalism have differed. Because liberalism both in Europe and in the United States was associated with massive change and social mobility, and the last century was fluid both in the new world and the old, the term "liberal" has been used with reckless abandon. Unfortunately, not much thought has been given to the differing points of departure and to the contrary directional features of social evolution in Europe/Canada and in the United States. They had started at vastly differing points on the socio-ideological spectrum — Europe on the far right about 1000 A.D., and America on the far left in 1776. When one says that America subsequently shifted rightward, one means rightward *in a liberal context*. The American right, in other words, was still far to the left, relatively speaking, of the European left, even as the latter evolved in the nineteenth century.

Nineteenth century America was, moreover, characterized by ongoing political reforms often encouraged by progressive, western frontier interests: the Jeffersonians, the Jacksonians, the free-soil Lincolnian Republicans, the Populists. These movements represented a reassertive strain of classical liberalism out of which the unique American conservative concept arose: in this century with growing governmental involvement in the United States, reform has ceased, in fact, to be a reassertive leftward tendency but has become just the opposite, a rightward one, which Americans do not recognize. Blinded by the notion of change as reform and liberalization, Americans have not come to grips with the conceptual significance in the altered socio-ideological direction between the last century and this century. Because of the ingrained sense of a necessary association of change, liberalism, modernity, and progress with the traditional left, it has not been recognized that in the United States the relative concepts of "liberalism" and "conservativism" have reversed, with the former favouring state activity and the latter disavowing it, unlike Europe/Canada. In other words, the European/Canadian mentality perceives the *totality* of the Western historical evolution with its associated socio-ideological spectrum and can trace to its feudal origins a sense of things "conservative". Because Americans have nothing comparable in their historical-ideological perspective, they trace only to the liberal divorcement of 1776 and now term this classical liberalism as "conservative". The Revolution of 1776 destroyed the American sense of historical direction based on Europe and, consequently, the terms "liberal" and "conservative" have come to represent almost exactly opposite notions in Europe/Canada on one hand and in the United States on the other.

XII

It would be appropriate at this point to indicate several of the more salient factors constituting the eclipse of classical liberalism and its replacement in the United States by a unique pluralism. One factor has been the growing sense of minority rights, of ethnicity and/or race, of special interests which often have been associated with a class-economic emphasis. This automatically encourages, not the classical liberal idea of a universal humanity, but rather a contrary notion of society constituted by limited, specific groups such as blacks or various ethnics, women, children, labour, unions, business and so forth. One cannot erect special allegedly "humanistic" and "liberal" laws to defend such limited interests for the very legal gesture of so doing divides society and confers a fully corporate aura. The Fourteenth Amendment to the American Constitution attempted to provide equal protection under the laws, a decidedly liberal gesture although enforcement was uneven. Applications of special laws have opened the door to the onerous problem of reverse discrimination. What inspires such "reforming" zeal is the American inability to discern the curious reversal of liberalism and conservativism in the United States and the lingering love affair with truly liberal ideals, their sense of justice equated with civil rights and broadened more recently to "human rights". Acts of exclusivity, irrespective of intent, only serve to undermine the individualistic substance of liberalism for, *de facto*, the concept of minority rights stands in direct opposition to the concept of universal rights.

With the eclipse of traditional monolithism has come an equally sharp check to the almost metaphysical sense of American popular purpose once termed Manifest Destiny. The East Asian Wars crushed the will of the conscript armies; the new professional army is an attempt to remove public opinion from the military imperative. The same socio-ideological fragmentation accords with the highly sophisticated and diverse economy of the United States. Liberalism was originally based on the farmer and the artisan: the economy has been increasingly fractured by various industries, by differing levels of competence, training, professionalism, management and unionism, and governmental interference. Segments of the economy can now function largely to the exclusion of other segments. The earlier, largely agrarian economic sameness has passed, to be replaced by business, industrial and governmental hierarchies, all of which are engendering both a hitherto unknown rigidity and a new sense of limited purpose. What the foregoing indicates when translated into politics is that the classical liberal notion of broad consensus in public life based on common (liberal) values, is fading, even in regard to fundamental issues, and a new fixity of limited attitudes is growing in strength.

One might also point to the divergence in the role of the city in the liberalizing period and in the corporate-liberal period. The European city had been the instrument of destruction for feudal corporatism; currently, many large American cities are *de facto* denying liberalism. Their ghettos have placed a large bloc of people outside the market economy and, given crime rates in certain areas, have instituted a virtual plunder economy. The welfare mechanism is, by its nature, incapable of inculcating liberal values and, quite the contrary, tends to instill a sense of dependence. That American city life in certain areas is running contrary to that in Europe and America between 1200 and 1900 A.D. may be traced to the initial failure to integrate minorities into the mainstream of American life; segregation has meant that minorities as distinct communities remained illiberal when the liberal dynamo was in full operation.

Not surprisingly, the recent corporate-liberal age has reinforced the distinctiveness of minorities. The traditional mechanisms by which minorities have been liberalized — a monetary economy, the free market, schools, political party patronage — appear unable to cope because corporate-liberalism has already altered their traditional functions. Even the workplace fails in this regard. It has long been a common belief in the West that liberalism has been associated with the genesis of industrialism, and from this it has been inferred that liberalism is essential to maintaining industrial society. What was necessary to germinal industrialization — individualistic inventive entrepreneurialism — is not only unnecessary for its advanced organized/hierarchical state but probably constitutes an inhibition to the sophisticated organization required by the new corporate socio-economic entities.

The shattering of monolithic liberalism has brought drift into American life. Lack of a popularly comprehended purpose is a genuine crisis for the United States: pluralism elsewhere is leading society down familiar ideological paths, but for America it is truly a distinct departure. The Revolution of 1776 has burned the bridges of retreat. At the same time, however, corporatism is jeopardizing the classical liberal ideals on which the Republic of 1776 was established. It has become as difficult for America to proceed as to retreat: hence, a curious impasse.

XIII

Pluralism appears to be superficially similar in Canada, Europe, and the United States, for in each the notion of socio-ideological exclusivity has become stronger. But a glance at the point of socio-ideological departure indicates that the foundations of pluralism in Europe/Canada and in the United States were quite distinct. The conventional perception of history as a singular, linear, leftward, modernizing progression in the general context of Western Civilization — an issue to be investigated in the chapter following — no longer suffices. The concepts associated with historical inquiry, whether socialistic, Marxist or liberal, have involved the related notions of universality and progress and/or modernity. By conventional definition, these were regarded as being conceptually on the left, the degree of leftward comprehension depending on whether one's perspective was liberal or socialist/Marxist. But because the United States was founded as the universal society and its subsequent general socio-ideological direction has been rightward, should not the concept of progress and/or modernity be reevaluated? If modernity has involved a strong liberal strain, then those in the United States most closely associated with classical liberalism (read: American conservativism, the western frontier reform/progressive tradition) have tended to be most suspicious of the ("modern") complex structures in government, business and industry. Paradoxically, American progress and/or modernity (if such it be) is endangering the liberal ideals on which the universal society has been based and is undermining the anti-feudal historical perception which has imbued the Republic with its popular dynamism. As America tends rightward threatening to undo the Revolution of 1776, so does the drift undermine the conventional concepts of modernity, liberalism, progress, and history which had formed a unique interlocking monolithic unity.

In conclusion, several points may be stated: pluralism is superficially and deceptively similar in various Western societies and an examination of its origins, structured conceptually, is necessary for revelation of its various distinctive qualities. The liberal perspective with its associated epistemology based on empiricism has not been an adequate mechanism for investigating pluralism and its "directional" features. Secondly, pluralism in the West has two basic forms, the corporate-liberal American and the feudalistic European/Canadian. Thirdly, for Europe the feudalistic revival constitutes a retreading of ideologically familiar territory; for Canada, apparently replicating the European example, there is cause for concern as the divergent forces of the "old order" compete for power and, in so doing, inadvertently menace the country's existence. For the United States, the progressive/modern order of 1776 is retreating before a unique pluralistic form about which consequences may not even be speculated. The concept of an essentially unified, progressive/modern Western Civilization does not appear to accord with reality as the constituent parts fragment.

Chapter Four:

Nationalism, Liberalism, and History

I

In the Anglo-American world, the central integrating socio-ideological force has been nationalism, which has been totally integrated with the liberal political economy. There has been an unwarranted assumption — both by various liberals and various Marxists — of the similarity of Canada to the Anglo-American world. But nationalism has a quite different translation in the liberalistic societies than in such pluralistic and illiberal societies as Canada.

There has often been an unfortunate tendency to think of nationalism in communitarian terms, a view which has failed to assign adequate significance to its liberal dimension in certain (but not all) societies. What has been confused is the distinction between communitarianism or collectivism on one hand and a commonly-held ideology on the other — a necessary distinction. Liberalism drew people together, creating national communities by ingraining a common ideology, a situation some observers consider paradoxical given its stress on atomistic individualism. But stress on the individual in no way precludes a national community or a nation state. Great Britain and the United States were not communitarian or collectivist, at least until the end of the last century.

The rise of ethnicity in eastern and central Europe provided various common ideologies for specific groupings of people who, too, gathered together into viable communities. But the social effect of an ethnically based ideology differed markedly from liberalism in creating communities truly communitarian, in that they stressed the predominance of the (ethnic) group rather than the individual. Liberalism and ethnicity both gave rise to political-constitutional structures that appeared *deceptively* similar and, consequently, both have been designated, rather uncritically, as "national" societies. But irrespective of the "national" designation, circumstance has placed both societies at opposite ends of the socio-ideological spectrum. That being so, this chapter aims to ascertain the historical basis of the socio-ideological spectrum as it relates to Western Civilization and, in the following chapter, to define the relative conceptual position of Canada on the spectrum.

II

Nationalism has always had emotional manifestations with an infinite variety of ramifications. That is part of the problem: one cannot precisely measure the scope of the values or their emotional strength. Perhaps the whole emphasis in approaching nationalism is incorrect. Perhaps historical inquiry should deal less with the nebulous and more with the concrete. One should not deal so much with something called nationalism as one should with nation building. The process by which the nation state was erected has been the all important factor, especially in those areas where its emergence has been of direct significance to the socio-ideological evolution of Canada. By way of analogy, the discussion of liberalism above has been directed less at the philosophical level than at the functional level. The same should be true of inquiries into nationalism whose functional objective must obviously be to create a nation state.

It sometimes has been suggested that all contemporary countries are nation states. Such a view is too casual. It is being suggested here that two distinct types of state structures have emerged in the West — the illiberal linguistic ethnic and the liberal national. Each arose out of a distinct tradition. What has obscured this fundamental divergence of the two traditions has been the erection of state structures. "States" these political units all have been; "nations" they all have not been. In the west, loyalty has been directed at the nation, the state being its extension. Further east, the state alone has been more demanding and consequently becomes the recipient of loyalty. Nor, one suspects, has language been an essential ingredient in the nation-building process in the West. It is true, of course, that following their successful Revolution, the Americans "Americanized" their English.[1] But this could be regarded as the logical and necessary prerequisite to the erection of a viable (liberal) society; it was not a persistent concern as self-sustaining as the imperatives of a distinct ethnicity. In a liberal society, language, along with religious and ethnic concerns, tends to be a secondary rather than a primary factor in the pantheon of values.

Nor, by its very nature, can liberalism be tolerant, for liberalism has a closed system of coherent values. By way of contrast, the so-called "nationalisms" of central Europe lack the fundamental benevolence basic to the more westerly liberal-mercantile peoples which actually mitigates the potential excesses of linguistic and ethnic expression. This is why, instead of the relatively humanistic, tolerant Scots-English relationship which has bestowed individualized economic benefits, there has been among the various ethnic communities of central and eastern Europe a deep, pervading antagonism based on complete misunderstanding. Such antagonism has historical causes, both genuine and false, but without individualized economic benefits to forestall it by a process of social integration and ideological homogenization, mutual community antagonisms surfaced. In other words, had money an educating opportunity in central Europe comparable to that in the West, its common monetary language may well have alleviated the lack of communication inherent in the ethnic languages by providing *individuals* with a common mercantile-liberal value system.

Rousseau helped to provide the intellectual stimulus to nationalism: he elevated emotion over logic and reason; he respected small homogeneous, sharply delimited communities; he promoted the concept of popular sovereignty which united the nation and the state. What spread the seeds of Rousseau's nationalism into fertile soil was the French Revolution. Libertarian ideas declined beyond the French frontier as the concept of the individual was subordinated to that of the community. Surely one must ask why central Europe so fully embraced Rousseau's philosophy when the West did not? What saved the West was the long tutelage of five centuries of indigenous liberalization originating in monetary commerce. The West did, of course, export to central Europe its liberalistic notions, but could not export its slowly evolved functional liberal ideology bearing indigenously developed legal and political institutions. Language and ethnicity rather than mercantile and liberal values became associated with state building in central Europe. Western nationalism was based on propertied individualism expressed through representative institutions; liberalism subordinated ethnic and linguistic values within such national contexts as Great Britain and the United States. Central European "nationalisms" shattered the pluralistic empires of that area into exclusive ethnic states which more often than not subordinated the individual and his property to community interests. In other words, what Rousseau had done was to articulate values already existing in central Europe, which accounts for its favourable response to small, non-Imperial communities.

Further to the east in Russia, the traditional borderland of Western Civilization, one finds the ultimate epitome of an illiberal system. There, state authority had never permitted a feudal system with its localized political-military power and the strongly ingrained concept of individualized contractual obligation. Nor did a powerful commercial state accompany the Muscovite revival of the fifteenth century like that of tenth century Kiev whose commercial class had embraced — according to some estimates[2] — one seventh of the population. By the seventeenth century, Russia had become a land of excessive taxation, currency debasement, inflation, urban depopulation, and the importation of foreign technical know-how. By the twentieth century neither nobles, nor peasants, nor mercantile, nor nascent industrial interests had developed any pronounced indigenous tradition of constitutionally enshrined rights. The Russian Revolution (to use the conventional terminology) completed the destruction of what had been, in the West, the two predominant classes, the potentially liberalistic mercantile-industrial interests and the long-declining nobility. Since the restructured and reinvigorated Russian state was henceforth limited by neither an exclusive (noble) interest nor a potentially popular one, the traditional Russian socio-political order emerged, in a Bolshevik guise, far on the right, overawing and subordinating the ethnic pluralism of the former Tsarist empire. The subsequent excursion into monolithic Stalinism was the logical outcome of the long-standing evolution toward centralized authoritarianism and state supremacy.

In feudal days, the area extending from central Europe to England exhibited enormous diversity. As the mercantile influence grew stronger from east to west, interacting with the legal and political systems, so did liberalizing attitudes severely alter a once-common society, especially in the West. The nineteenth century saw the fruition of this development which produced two state structures in Europe not generally distinguished, the ethnic and the national. To translate this into another frame of reference, central Europe had been introduced to the print medium and by 1919 had successfully created several ethnic states based on the vernacular. The West, having been earlier subjected to the technology of monetary commerce, did utilize print technology but was never "ideologicalized" by it; that is to say, was never subordinated to the supremacy of linguistic imperatives. A common *schema* often associates language and nationality: but liberal bourgeois nationalism arose in the West where the vernacular had no especially liberal associations. Both conceptually and geographically, expansive liberalism and nationalism on one hand, and exclusive language and ethnicity on the other hand, have been diametrically opposite.

Translated into the terminology of political science, this means that western liberalism has been leftward and that as one moves eastward across Europe, the socio-political structures, increasingly illiberal, have been also more rightward, halting only with Russia, the most illiberal and reactionary of all. Canadian society, of course, has never related to the geographical references but has, to some degree, accorded with the conceptual ones. Because of French, British and American influences, Canada has, by way of contrast, taken on a veneer of Western refinement far more successfully than Russia has. Associations with the English and French languages and Canadian desires for the gadgets of the liberal industrial societies have all tended to place Canada superficially within the context of Western Civilization. But this is quite deceptive and obscures the fact that deep psychological and ideological differences based on distinctive values have set Canada off from the source lands of that Civilization. The ideological "iron curtain" which has separated Canadians from their Anglo-American and French foundations has been quite as deep as that which distinguishes the Russians. This is not to say, of course, that Canada and Russia are similar societies, for obviously they are not. But both do exhibit, in contradistinction to the Anglo-American world, a rightward pluralistic tradition (ie anti-liberal, deferential to state authority, elitist, non-popular). In Russia, this process has run to its logical conclusion; in Canada this process, which is currently associated with the introduction of "Westernization" and modernity in the liberal Anglo-American sense, is just now being faced.

The concept of a socio-political spectrum is not a fantasy of political science but is an historical reality based on the western-national-liberal and the eastern-ethnic-linguistic fragmentation of Europe. In terms of the socio-political spectrum, the liberal left has been the Anglo-American world while the right has constituted its antithesis, central Europe and, ultimately, the Russian monolith, where the state structure is constructed to contain and suppress fragmenting (ethnic) tendencies. Three constant criteria have governed the socio-political spectrum — the concepts of the state, the community, the individual. What has varied along the spectrum has been the relationship between the three concepts, authoritarianism and minimal civil rights in the east, and liberal democracy and maximal civil rights in the West. The spectrum has been, moreover, relatively constant in time: collectivism and illiberalism have always characterized the east/right. In the east, without comparable concepts of change and progress indige-nously ingrained, society has not undergone *fundamental* ideo-logical evolution. This is why, despite the so-called "Revolution" in Russia, what really reemerged was an enhanced version of the traditional authoritarian illiberalism in Marxist guise. The west/ left has of course been far more flexible, having been based on the (advance and retreat of) concepts of progress and change: despite its liberalistic interlude, Great Britain has run full cycle by virtue of the revival of fragmenting ethnicity and socialism/estatism; the United States, as previously noted, while retaining a classical liberal strain finds itself characterized by a new, unfamiliar corporatism and special interests.

What one must always remember is the constancy of the socio-ideological spectrum bound by leftward propertied individualism and rightward communitarianism and/or collectivism. This helps to explain how rightward societies can move abruptly "leftward" (to use conventional terminology) to some brand of Marxism. This "leftward" shift never, in fact, occurs: concep-tually, such societies "side step", so to speak, within the context of the highly diversified right, from one type of illiberalism to another. Shifts across the spectrum from illiberalism to liberalism (and back again) are only possible after a very lengthy period of evolution. The introduction of new, alleged "leftward" or socialistic philosophies in the nineteenth century have not broadened the functional socio-political spectrum on the left. The effective leftward limit of the functional spectrum was probably best expressed by the very liberal Articles of Confederation in the United States which bordered on chaos. The Mexican and Canadian limitations to the physical expansion of the Republic denied its leftward metaphysical potential, conceptually speaking, and helped lessen, constitutionally and politically, its unstable tendency towards universality. This contributed to the eventual transformation of the United States into a genuine nation state, which, as a concept, implies fixity and stability. The final act in this evolution, of course, has just recently been played out in the twentieth century East Asian wars.

This liberal limitation of the functional left of the socio-ideological spectrum had several causes. Atomistic individualism, by its very nature, permitted no further leftward social evolution: after all, the individual could not be further atomized or subdivided. The only alternative to individualism was communitarianism or collectivism of some type — the right, not the left. Also, liberal systems represent, *de facto*, the effective limit to socio-ideological homogeneity. Marx, of course, disagreed; he perceived a further and more complete communized homogeneity on an international scale. But that, as it has turned out, was pure theory and rhetoric, not historical reality. *Functional* Marxism has not been leftward because it claims to speak for a very specific and limited group — the urban working class — a factor which makes it as limited and exclusive as was each of the three estates of pre-revolutionary France. Marxism and the philosophies it has fathered have, consequently, not been popular and accessible to the degree that liberalism has. Where some brand of Marxism has come to predominate over the past six decades, retrenching along fairly traditional ideological (ie rightward) lines seems to follow.

In fact, the universality of Marxism has been eclipsed as Marxism itself has been adopted by illiberal — and often ethnic, regional and/or "national" — variations of pluralism. What Marxism has lacked in its geographically successful areas is the ingraining interplay of accessible popular materialism, the sheer immediacy of an inculcating mechanism such as land and capital. The lack of such instant material benefits rendered Marxism spurious in terms of a functional socio-ideological reality. Where Marxism gained ground, it did so through intellectual elites, and therefore never totally replaced the predominant indigenous ideologies. Marxist theory built on both liberalism and feudalism from which Marxism attempted to divorce itself. Because the motive force of history was, in Marxist theory, an economically inspired struggle between upper or wealthy classes and lower or dispossessed ones, the theory of Marxism dictated a class struggle which was expounded in universal terms. But the struggle was limited in time and its outcome was historically and "scientifically" predictable; the eschatological and deterministic quality of Marxist "history" reduced it to nothing more than secular theology. Theory in such a system outweighed dispassionate empirical test. That rendered Marxism not a functionally leftward extension of liberalism but a regressive rejection of it. The far left — left of liberalism — has remained an elusive Marxist ideal.

III

History was, so to speak, invented in the liberalizing West with its integrating and ideologically monolithic tendencies. For history with an unquestioned framework *de facto* liberal or rhetorically Marxist — both of which are leftward, one functionally, the other theoretically — the regression from the liberal left has, with pluralism of differing origins rampant everywhere, been almost impossible to deal with in a conceptual fashion. History continues to attempt to interpret the retreat from liberalism and (American) universalism in terms of the same concepts that it has utilized in evaluating the anti-feudal evolution from the tenth to the nineteenth century. But the growth of European/Canadian neo-feudalism and the recent corporate-liberalism of the United States cannot be made to fit such a model because the traditional and simple concept of leftward-progressive history is just not valid any longer. A new comprehension is essential for conceptual clarity.

The study of the past has really only made sense in the last 500 years or so as the randomness of the liberal evolution from feudal ideological fixity encouraged a search for stability and certainty based on points of liberal departure and subsequent evolution. Rightward societies, by their nature, are not especially adept at historical thinking because they lack the perspectives necessary for such comprehension. Time, for one, becomes too "collapsed" on the right because corporatism, whether medieval or contemporary, is essentially the same and, consequently, does not appear *historically* distant: the mere time distance of a thousand years is not necessarily sufficient to engender an historical sense. This becomes more understandable if one graphically describes the functional socio-ideological and historical spectrum as an angle ($\angle$) with the leftward collapsing of the two spokes representing the integrating process, the terminus in monolithic liberalism; the increasing rightward distance between the spokes conveys the sense of a strengthening medieval and/or neo-feudal diversity.

Historical distance becomes a left-right consideration; expounded thus, history becomes, so to speak, an aspect of place on the socio-ideological spectrum.

The implications of this left-right divergence have been far-reaching for historical study because history has generally been perceived as a universal discipline. In fact, genuine history has been limited to societies essentially "modern" or Western which have journeyed the liberal(izing) path. Elsewhere the progressive assumptions of historical inquiry do not apply and what has passed for historical study has, more often than not, been subordinate to other more parochial and/or eschatological imperatives. Most parochial societies have learned the superficial dimensions of historical inquiry: its empiricism, its literary tradition, its (scientific) methodology. This has permitted the use of what passes for "history" as a blatant instrument of propaganda by parochial interests. If history in the West itself has largely been the handmaiden of liberalism and, by wearing liberal spectacles, one has been permitted only a singular (anti-corporate) view of the universe, then elsewhere historical epistemology has been enlisted blatantly in the service of even lesser ideologies. The decline of the universal imperative in the liberal heartland has, so to speak, left history without its original mission. Once, the Western peoples were truly historical; those elsewhere never were.

As Western man moved from the feudal ideology and became liberalized, a sense of the past permeated popular considerations. To the Englishmen who rebelled against British paternalism in America and then transformed the rebellion into revolution, there was a deep awareness — at least among the educated — of the distinctiveness of the Anglo-American tradition. The ideological-geographical distinction between the "new" world and the "old" encouraged a comparison with the socio-ideology from which Western man was evolving. The Glorious Revolution with its declared rejection of things feudal was less than a century old when the American Revolution occurred, and the French Revolution scarcely more than a century; the obvious holdovers from medieval feudalism were only destroyed in central and eastern Europe in the nineteenth century and the Ottoman Empire, itself essentially a medieval institution, lasted until the early twentieth century. But the very passing of the empirically obvious institutions of the old order in Europe has divorced Western Civilization from an intimate sense of its corporate-medieval origins. Modern man (read: Americanized, liberalized man) has been left without an indigenous sense of the past and has further lost all immediate comparative guideposts of his European past. And if a sense of the past diminishes, then a sense of history correspondingly fades.

Because the growth of liberalism in the West was associated with a sense of history, it seems only logical that the decline of individualistic liberalism should be directly related to a comparable erosion of historical vitality. The erosion of respect for history as a valid branch of knowledge may, in part, be traced to the intellectual reorientation to the post-industrial age or, more preferably from the ideological viewpoint, to the corporate liberal age. One need only glance at the necessary emphasis in such a society with its stress on management which aims to achieve overall defined objectives at some future time; the mechanisms of achievement are as fluid as the dynamic technology on which they rest. In this socio-ideological system, the randomness of classical liberalism with its mindless series of egalitarian relationships — often dictated by *laissez faire* economics — has passed away. Nor do the distinct limitations of medievalism with its fixed "eternal" Divine law, nor inevitable results based on "scientific" Marxism, with its forces of production, have any place in corporate-liberalism. The new socio-ideological fluidity as one moves from classical monolithic liberalism engenders genuine possibilities: certainly American ideology is not sterile as George Grant, who decries the poverty of American liberalism, has warned. But corporate-liberalism does detract, admittedly, from the value of history as a valid object of study.

Liberal man (modern man) was decidedly historical; corporate-liberal man (contemporary American man) has become less historically aware than his forebearers. This denotes a pronounced departure from the universal-liberal society and from its unique view of the universe. The new society has become increasingly devoted to an attempt, not to comprehend its original divorcement from feudalism, but rather to master its future. Just as historical inquiry served classical liberalism, so has futurology, management, and administration emerged as the handmaiden of the corporate/business world and of government with their complexities and efforts to master given environments. This new orientation symbolizes the transformation from classical liberalism, which emphasizes the Rights of Man in a potentially functional universal society, to corporate-liberalism which still adheres to the attractive notions of classical liberalism. But corporate-liberalism, in fact, places Man in the functionally limiting structures of business, industry, and government — all emergent bureaucracies which subordinate the individual to various overlapping and complex collectivities.

Two centuries ago, no people were more historically literate and popularly conscious of their English traditions, their uniqueness in the world, and of the general anti-feudal drift of history as it related to the "blessings" of liberty than the Americans. The American tradition was part of the overarching British tradition which was simultaneously evolving and which was rejecting narrow corporate and ethnic exclusivity. In the final analysis, however, America became the universal society rather than Great Britain: ethnicity and corporatism were never totally eclipsed in the British Isles and in its remaining colonial dependencies. The American Revolution, by integrating the thirteen original colonies into a new state structure which denied itself colonies, adopted the overarching notions of the universalizing "British" sense (even if, rhetorically, the American rebels had spoken of "English" rights).

But American success was self-destructive: American monolithism with its attendant ideological certainty has militated against continuing historical literacy on a broad scale. From being once the most popularly informed and historically articulate people, the Americans have become far less so. They have lost a comprehension of the uniqueness of their history and liberal institutions. With the passing of history as a popular field for intellectual exercise has come its transmutation in the schools into "social studies" in which jumbled references from the past are curiously intermixed with the jargon of different disciplines. The result is often an incomprehensible marriage of isolated "concepts" and bits and pieces of the past, all of which is a far cry from the initial historical function to integrate the rich diversity of the past into a comprehensible system.

Alternatively, at the highest levels, history has become more specialized and narrow and, consequently, less popular. The professionalism of the historical guild has engendered an elitism at variance with the popular liberalism out of which the historical craft first arose and whose universal purpose served to ennoble Man. In the wake of the passing of history has come a detachment between the professionals with their limited perspectives and the masses. What has become of historical study — its transmutation into social studies and its professional exclusivity — is itself symptomatic of the retreat of the universal ideal of the United States and its once unquestioned ideology. The Rights of Man concept is no longer viable and current efforts to promote "human rights" around the world probably represent the infamous "last gasp" of liberalism. After all, functionally, liberalism is retreating.

Like some of the pre-modern societies which it denigrated, classically liberal America assumed an eternity based on the fixity of immutable truth whose comprehension was logically self-evident to any rational human being. Such a perspective rejects as unnecessary history as an ongoing discipline because things worth knowing are empirically self-evident to the ordinary (common, rational) man. Once necessary to structure and to set the universal state into motion in accord with its popular ideology, historical comprehension subsequently lost its *raison d'être* for it did not appear to be essential to maintain the imperatives of that state. The monolithism and fixity of the liberal ideology for two centuries has devoided history as a *total* encounter because historical inquiry has not been permitted to question the assumed essentials of the liberal ideology. From this, in turn, derived such distortions as the "end of ideology" movement in which modern liberal society regarded itself as the ultimate rendering of Mankind; something quite similar has long animated Marxist thought with its pretensions to a modernity coterminous with a universal proletarian society.

The conventional linear theories of history — liberal and

Marxist — have assumed that flux in the sense of social evolution has been total — economic, political, religious, military, constitutional, and ideological. But flux is only the superficial expression of all physical life, the satisfaction of its wants and the creation of various systems — economic, military constitutional, and so forth — to satisfy those desires. The identification of the tension between change and relative constancy in objective historical reality is worthwhile in order to ascertain the limits of historical study as epistemology. The liberalistic conceptual framework has been inadequate because of its necessary associations with superficialities. History as epistemology must inquire into the fundamentals which reveal a relative constancy over long periods of time; the transient superficialities — constitutionalism, politics, economics, culture, religion — are only guides to a more fundamental dimension, not ends in themselves. What the fundamental aspect, the socio-ideology, does is to permit a conceptual approach as opposed to a narrative-chronological rendering which is necessarily specific and limited in character.

Historical epistemology has been assumed to be virtually anti-Platonic, in that the Platonic ideal consisted of a singular constant reality exclusive of the physical and dimensional vagaries of space and time. At the other (theoretical) extreme has been Marxism. It is based on the materialistic concept of flux, movement, change and evolution in a "progressive" direction which eschatologically denies that critical empiricism, generally associated with "knowledge" in a truly leftward (liberal) ideology. Classical liberalism divorces the perceiver from the object to be comprehended. This distance between perceiver and object permits the mind to "compact" specific events in time and space advantageously, to seek out common circumstance or fundamentals, to create in the present mind a subjective notion of the past — an historical conceptualizing, so to speak. Such a "space-time compaction" or conceptualization is a constant, and, by extension, historical comprehension should aim to ascertain the relative and essential constancy on which social superficiality is based. This comprehension of history does not dismiss change, but it does seek clues in the flux which are political, economic, religious, and military to help identify and explain the functional ideological fundamentals.

The fixity of concepts in space and time renders them logically consistent because conceptualizations represent abstractions structured from varied and often seemingly contradictory events and circumstances. The mental process whereby such jumbled variety in the past is elevated to history and/or ideology required the victory of classical liberalism with its rejection of feudal chaos, its devotion to order, and its respect for rationality. The very act of historical conceptualization is an act of rationality: by making the past (and present) comprehensible through "universal" fixed, timeless, and non-geographical conceptual guidelines, all the activities of humankind past and present have been rendered more comprehensible than is possible in the vast sweep of sheer linear chronology.

Only in the United States, with no ingrained values of a contrary sort to obstruct expansive liberalism, did the historical process move to a completion — from which the Americans have since retreated. Elsewhere, change has involved a "side-stepping" consistent with traditional value systems, so that "historical" flow was not progressive or linear. These social types have been limited in their perception of space and time, and have been devoted to certain geographic locations, a devotion often encouraged through (pseudo-)historical perceptions conditioned by ethnic, religious, theological and/or eschatological views. "History" as a simple study of the past did not liberate the minds of the parochial/ethnic/eschatological people because historical theory as developed in the West was specifically designed to accommodate the liberal world-view. This is why the socio-ideological ("historical") "side-stepping" so characteristic of most of the world's people has gone unrecognized. It is also why the collapse of the central and east European empires in this century and the achievement of Canadian autonomy from Britain have been falsely regarded as a progressive, modernizing events when, in fact, ingrained ideologies remained intact. "Nationalism" has been largely a term (a "modern" term) which has obscured the retention of ideological constants, and, consequently, to investigate nationalism one must look at, and then beyond, its obvious superficialities: the mere occupation of real estate, the stated aspirations of cultural groups, the varied manifestations that evoke mass emotion. One comes to a much better grasp of nationalism not by studying any particular group but by coming to grips with the foundational socio-ideological spectrum out of which differing "nationalisms" arose.

IV

The significance of the foregoing to Canadian historical inquiry, and to Western political concepts generally, cannot be down-graded: the two concepts of nationalism which appear in Canadian history — the liberal and the ethnic — are not analogous concepts and ought not be so treated. The so-called nationalism of French-speaking Quebec has obviously not been like the nationalism of the United States, since the two are at opposite ends of the socio-political spectrum. Anglo-American nationalism was expansive, welcoming diverse ethnic groups into its state structure; ethnicity has been limiting and exclusive, restricting those who appear different, destroying state structures that defy or inhibit ethnicity. Despite its theoretical claim to universality, the functional reality of Marxism has made it the logical ally of ethnic, exclusive, illiberal structures. The tendency among liberal and Marxist historians to regard history as a linear sequence moving from right to left — a concept with only limited historical application — is inadequate because not all societies may be judged in terms of left-to-right (or right-to-left) shifts.

Some societies such as Canada, Austria-Hungary and its successor states, tsarist Russia and The Soviet Union, and pre-revolutionary France have evolved within a rightward context making it virtually impossible to conceptualize their histories in traditional right to left (or liberalistic and/or Marxist) terms. In western Europe, too, liberalism has been in rightward retreat. The iron curtain in Europe does not at present so much divide the Russian-Soviet Empire from western Europe as it divides the more universal and historical peoples from the traditional parochial ones. In that sense, the iron curtain is being pushed back to the Atlantic Ocean. The geographical area in which popular historical comprehension is possible has been steadily restricted and limited and is even under attack in America, the heartland of that comprehension. Only America, detached from Europe for two centuries, retains the truly historical ability to shift on the left-right axis, but even that capacity appears to be passing. As the United States becomes increasingly corporate-liberal (with emphasis on the first adjective), America, too, will likely become more entrapped by "side-stepping" power struggles among large structures and interest groups, and less devoted to the imperatives of classical individualism.

To sum up, the conventional left-right concept is valid in certain limited circumstances in Western history, but further refinement of the concept is necessary to account for societies which have not evolved in a left-right fashion. Instead of the standard liberal and Marxist historical "straight line" sequence with the feudalistic/tory right, the liberal centre, and the socialis-tic/Marxist left, it has been proposed to conceive of an angle pointing leftward on its side: $\angle$. The angle represents ideological diversity within the context of Western Civilization. The apex of the angle ideologically represents societies which are or have been liberal, individualistic, or homogeneous, as characterized by post-revolutionary England-Great Britain, the United States, and France. As far as the United States is concerned, one should conceive it as the leftward extension of the Western socio-ideological spectrum, now "detached" as America retreats rightward from classical liberalism. Its retreat does not constitute a return to European toryism, but does represent a new departure into the socio-ideological unknown. Aside from the unique American situation, as one moves rightward along the socio-ideological spectrum certain characteristics become more intense: pluralism, diversity, often ethnicity, collectivism and communi-tarianism — all of which have always distinguished central and eastern Europe. Given that the failure of liberalism in central and eastern Europe produced a "national" social type quite different from the classical Anglo-American, one must now examine the national effect in Canada which also rejected functional classical liberalism.

Chapter Five:

(Anti-)Canadianism and Popular Canadianism

I

What is conventionally termed nationalism has, like so many other concepts, never been indigenous to Canada. Consequently, one must first examine Canadian evolution in the light of an alien term and its associated notions in order to place Canada properly on the socio-ideological spectrum relative to other Western societies. This requires an analysis of (anti-)Canadianism. Secondly, despite the erosion of classical liberalism in the United States, that ideology continues to radiate its enormous energy into Canada by virtue of geographical proximity. The transformation of the universal society into a more truly national one has substantial implications for Canada. To facilitate the inquiry, the first sections of this chapter will address the problem of (anti-)Canadianism and the rest will be devoted to popular Canadianism and its relationship to American liberalism.

II

The traditional idea that (Upper and/or English) Canadian society had to choose between either Britain or the United States — a fundamental concept of the liberal and conservative-liberal schools of Canadian history — is simply not valid in the ideological sense. The crisis of identity and nationalism in Upper Canada was even more complicated than most commentators have realized.

Between 1774 and 1776 the identity of another North American society was satisfactorily resolved. But the problem of the 1770s had only two well-defined options — independence or subordination. In the Thirteen Colonies, independence had represented a difference, not in kind but in degree; it constituted a shift away from an emphasis on "English rights" with their lingering notions of socio-political exclusiveness to "American rights" with more popular connotations. The Upper Canadian situation, given its pluralism, exhibited three possibilities and was thus infinitely more complex than the American had been. The Family Compact and the Tories were anti-liberal and anti-nationalistic; their entire function involved the mobilization of resources to prevent a recurrence of the radical indigenous liberal nationalism that had, in 1776, upset the British Empire. Tory empathy for the Imperial authority derived in large measure from the conviction that they constituted the British nationality in North America.

At the other extreme were the Radicals who had a more localistic Upper Canadian emphasis but, for reasons already noted, were neither able to divorce themselves from American associations nor to symbolize and inspire a distinct Upper Canadian liberal nationalism. Indeed, the very Radicals who claimed to be most representative of the popular interest in the province were also most divorced from the masses. What had made the most extreme of these Upper Canadian Reformers into revolutionaries was the erosion of the political method by which reform could be effected. A Tory dominated Assembly in 1831 had removed the very basis for reform by conceding a permanent civil list; thereafter, high officials and some civil servants were paid independently of supply voted by the House of Assembly. While this gesture was certainly in the Upper Canadian tradition of strengthening the executive, it also provided the basis for revolutionary extremism. The permanent civil list eliminated, for Upper Canadian Reformers schooled in the intricacies of British constitutional history, the one method — a financial-constitutional struggle — by which Englishmen had attained their civil rights. If the basic method of moderate reform was thus eliminated, then the most dedicated Reformers had but one alternative, to follow the popular method and political model of the extreme left, the revolution and the republic, respectively.

It has been claimed that the Reformers represented a genuine American-influenced democratic ferment which demanded provincial self government. Although one may easily indicate several points of similarity — the demand for voting by ballot, the abolition of primogeniture, the elimination of excessive economic privilege, the demand for easy credit for small business — the *sum* ideological effect was anti-democratic and illiberal. Nor, consequently, was any (Upper) Canadian sense of nationalism developed. William Lyon Mackenzie and his extremists had failed to grasp the difference between the Thirteen Colonies in 1776 and Upper Canada in 1837 in regard to revolutionary potential, although conditions may have seemed, superficially, quite similar. Several essential revolutionary factors were absent from Upper Canada in 1837.

In England, in the Thirteen Colonies in the 1770s, and in France in the 1780s, the business community was committed to the opposition of governmental policies injurious to its interests. By way of illustration, the American frontier interests had not rebelled after the detrimental Proclamation of 1763 but only after the Intolerable Acts of 1774 had generated eastern mercantile hostility against Britain. Lieutenant Governor Bond Head's action in 1836 — the withholding of revenue from public works — was a clear reversal of the liberal British tradition wherein the Commons, not the Crown, withheld revenue to the ultimate benefit of ever more popular interests. Liberalism was thereby associated with nationalism (ie anglicism; "the rights of Englishmen"). Of course, the reverse process was encouraged in Upper Canada where the resulting depression in 1836 and 1837 did not draw the businessmen, who were often Tories, into the Radical camp; for them, the solution was anything but a rebellion that would further disrupt the state, the largest provincial spender. Not only the rebellious colonial tradition of 1774 with its appeal for English rights, but the very foundations of those rights achieved by the English Civil War and the Glorious Revolution were, at one stroke, rejected in 1836 and 1837. What was elsewhere eroding — the principle of royal prerogative — emerged victorious in Upper Canada. The counter-revolutionary victory of the Lieutenant-Governor's political party in the 1836 provincial election symbolically reintegrated the monarchical and prime ministerial offices. The popular (national) liberalizing advances of British constitutionalism since Robert Walpole had been virtually undone and were reinforced by the suppression of the 1837 Rebellion. The Radical programme had inadvertently destroyed any possibility for liberal nationalism in Upper Canada.

Another point to be made about the Upper Canadian identity crisis concerns the Moderate Reformers. They, like the Tories, had strong British associations from which they could not easily divorce themselves. The Moderates wished to anglicize (ie liberalize) the method of government, to shift authority to the provincial Executive Council which, in turn, would be drawn from and responsible to the majority in the Assembly. The Moderates were not disputing the concept of executive predominance but were interested in determining who, within the executive context, had final authority, the crown appointed Lieutenant-Governor or his colonial advisors, the Executive Council. When the Moderates had to choose during the 1837 Rebellion between a false appeal to things British and a sincere appeal to revolution based on the American model, that they would choose the former, a system involving executive predominance, was a foregone conclusion. Sometimes rebellious but never revolutionary, the slogan "the rights of Englishmen" best expressed the ideals of most Moderates: like the Radicals and the Tories, the Moderates had no especially "Canadian" tendencies.

Thus, the Upper Canadian socio-political spectrum had no genuine, indigenous Canadian options; the liberal left had

American connotations, the moderate centre and the right remained rhetorically British. At no point on the spectrum could a coherent, clearly identifiable Upper Canadian nationalism — liberal or otherwise — develop.

III

Hilda Neatby has taken a generalized view of nationalism among the French Canadians, suggesting that it originated with the British Conquest which stimulated and irritated the conquered. The American Revolution and the new Anglo-French war rendered anglicization impossible. What finally produced a "genuine" nationalism, in Neatby's view, was the isolation of the habitants from the British authorities, from the seigneurs, and from the loyalists, as well as the inability of the Church to recruit from the anti-revolutionary clergy of France. Forced into a defensive unity, the *Canadiens* absorbed the nationalism of the French Revolution.[1] What Neatby has done, of course, is to trace the rising sense of ethnicity. The external influences which contributed to this — the American and French Revolutions — although liberal in their indigenous environments, were clearly not so in Quebec. There, the individualistic ideals of revolution became community ones and extraterritorially-inspired liberalism gave way to something far more conservative: ethnicity.

Fernand Ouellet places the emergence of French-Canadian nationalism at the start of the nineteenth century and seems to believe that it was associated with a sense of ethnicity,[2] thereby agreeing with Donald Creighton that the Anglo-French conflicts before the 1780s had been social, not ethnic. In Ouellet's view, nationalism accompanied the emergence of the French Canadian bourgeoisie and liberal professions as a political force in Lower Canada. The bourgeoisie simultaneously developed a class consciousness which was coincidental with its nationalism, as a conservative expression of defensive hostility to those things which characterized English-speaking elements.

One cannot deny Ouellet's claim that the bourgeoisie articulated the discontent of the masses and that this took an ethnic form, although many complex socio-economic factors were involved. But we should not assume that such articulations were manifestations either of liberalism or nationalism. Most probably, they were manifestations of something more conservative than either. After all, even if nationalism is regarded as somewhat more conservative than liberalism, the former representing an exclusive social view, the latter a somewhat more general one, all ideologies on the socio-political spectrum are relative and both nationalism and liberalism, when compared to ethnicity, are relatively quite popular. It is conceded that Ouellet correctly identifies the contra-diction in French-Canadian thought — its liberal democratic pretensions on the left and its "nationalism" on the right — but what Ouellet fails to note is a further hiatus: that the functional ideology of French Canada was far more rightward than "nationalism". In other words, Ouellet has not appreciated the fact that French-Canadian society had not become "popularized" sufficiently before the Rebellion of 1837 for its functional ideology to provide a basis for genuine liberal nationalism.

The latter failed to emerge in French Canada because, unlike Anglo-America, the bourgeoisie and ("liberal"?) professions were not, ideologically, either a liberalizing or a national force. For one thing, the necessary machinery — a market economy — does not seem to have existed to assure the transmission of extra-ethnic liberal values to the *entire* Lower Canadian society. Instead of liberalism acting as an organic unifier and leveller, Lower Canadian society retained and strengthened its tendency toward "class" based on a growing awareness of linguistic-ethnic-economic distinctions. The (imported) ideologies of liberalism and nationalism had no indigenous functional reality in Lower Canada but were utilized to enshrine ever more deeply existing ethnic differences. The Rebellion of 1837 did not alleviate this situation because the victors, although prone to use the rhetoric of liberalism, did not symbolize or functionally utilize liberalism.

A problem confronting many investigators, including Ouellet, has been the assumption that a class-based ethnic consciousness in a bi-ethnic or a multi-ethnic society may be associated with liberalism and/or nationalism. This is not so. While it is true that the conscious expounding of concepts can reflect liberalistic rhetoric, the functional reality of any group, whether a minority or a majority within the total society, is such that it constitutes an exclusive interest. In short, far too much attention has been directed to the French Canadians or to the English-speaking interest rather than to the *totality* of Lower Canadian society. The political-constitutional community was not French Canadian or English Canadian but was Lower Canadian and, because of that, any analysis should not investigate the particular "nationalism" of a limited interest but rather Lower Canadian nationalism. Any sub-loyalty within the Lower Canadian jurisdiction was, ultimately, an infringement of a Lower Canadian sense of community and was, by definition, anti-nationalistic. This should help resolve the paradox of Lower Canada; namely, that one finds two ethnic interests both of which consciously contained liberal elements which may elsewhere have become nationalistic. But because of the translation which it received in Lower Canadian society, liberalism was used to sustain an ethnic-economic social division rather than to alleviate it. Lower Canada consequently remained a non-national society. And, of course, a functionally illiberal one.

The Imperial government had expected after the Conquest and, again, after the unsuccessful Rebellions of 1837, that the British Americans of Quebec/Lower Canada would serve as instruments of liberal national anglicization *vis-à-vis* the French Canadians. This was predicated on the quite unwarranted assumption that the British Americans were, at once, fundamentally Englishmen and liberal nationalists. Unfortunately for Imperial policy, the British-American commercial interests in Lower Canada had never developed any nationalistic empathy for the province. It represented unpleasant associations: the unfulfilled promise of the original anglicization policy of 1763, the injuries and injustices of the Quebec Act, the inadequacies of the Constitutional Act. Nor could the British Americans encourage any program of liberalism because it raised the danger of being swamped by the French Canadians. That the British Americans remained a non-industrial commercial class meant that they did not go the way of the American Federalists after 1812, when the latter began to invest heavily in such tangible assets as factories and real estate and thereby developed a nationalistic tendency consistent with western Jeffersonianism. The termination of preferential commercial status in the British Empire in the late 1840s and American Congressional action in the Drawback Acts led not to a gesture of self-reliant liberal localism like that of the Thirteen Colonies in 1774 but to the Annexation Manifesto which sought outright incorporation into the Republic. The proposed instrument of anglicization was, itself, neither anglicized, nor nationally aware, nor liberal.

The French-Canadian community had also developed deep aversions to the ideology of the liberal left. After 1760, the latter was appropriated, symbolically, by the arriving British merchants who thereby took upon themselves and their posterity all the latent hostilities of the habitants. There was disenchantment with leftward monetary economics, expressed through pre-Conquest inflation, post-Conquest partial default of the French government, and the later unhappy experience with revolutionary American paper. Nor were the politics of the left especially attractive, embodied as they were in the anglicization policy of 1763 and revolutionary Americanism, both of which threatened French Canada. With nothing to alleviate the initial hostility to the popular left, the population remained exclusive, continuing to exhibit "French" affinities long after the Conquest. That so disliked a Governor as Craig regarded them as French in manner, attachment, language, and religion may well have reinforced the tendency, despite Craig's own admission of their self-identification as *"la Nation Canadienne"* by 1810. Even the currency of post-revolutionary France was preferred in Lower Canada to British currency.[3] The Constitutional Act, intended as a liberal gesture, opened the way to an articulation, although not as assertion, of habitant values which, under the influence of the revolutionary quest for legal and social justice, were misdirected to ethnic and linguistic concerns. There developed, consequently, a very limited sense of community which simply could not embrace all Lower Canadians.

It is an axiom of liberal nationalism that a sense of common destiny among individuals must exceed the divisive, special interests of various groups of communities within the total society. Rather than a basic cohesive materialism broadly ingraining a common set of individualistic liberal values, both Lower Canadian communities like those of eastern and central Europe focused on ethnicity, language, religion and culture. The linguistically French feared the left as "English". The linguistically English, who included the Upper Canadians after 1840, were equally locked into an anti-American and, by logical extension, an anti-liberal and pseudo-English self-perception. There could never be a (truly liberal) Canadian nation state.

IV

Both liberal and conservative-liberal historians have tended to confuse the mere existence of Canada with its status as a nation state. For conservative-liberal historians, the nation was shaped by the east-west trade in staples, the real significance of which has been to define the extent of Canadian real estate. As Innis has pointed out, the agricultural bases of supply for the fur trade in Quebec, western Ontario, and British Columbia have become the agricultural areas of the Dominion. Similarly, Creighton has noted that the main problem of Canadian development, faced originally by the merchants in the eighteenth century, was the structuring of a continental society situated on the St Lawrence River and the Canadian Shield. The mere gathering-in of territory, it should be remembered, is essentially economic and political-constitutional, and does not necessarily involve an indigenous definition of ideology. Donald Creighton and his historical hero, Sir John A Macdonald, have recognized two goals of Canadian "nationhood": autonomy within the British Empire and a second nationality on the North American continent. On the other hand, the liberal school has regarded Canadian status, historically, as a colonial one *vis-à-vis* Britain; the road to national independence has been accomplished to the degree that Canada has emulated the United States in removing British influences. The unwarranted assumption in the latter instance has been that the rejection of Britain automatically brought about (or is in the process of bringing about) a national Canadian existence in the liberal tradition. Such as the Creightonians would merely reply that anti-British gestures opened the way to Americanization and recolonization, the "national" period, at best, having been of very short duration. For both schools, the central factors in claiming a Canadian nationality exists (or does not exist, whatever the case may be) have been mostly restricted to the politics and economics of a three-way drama involving Canada, Britain, and the United States.

Neither the liberal school nor the conservative-liberal school has given proper attention to a national Canadian genesis, which has been far more complex than the consolidation of Britain and the United States. Unlike Canada, they were not "trapped" politically and economically between two alternative powers. In the United States and Great Britain, the ideological definition of nationality was rendered much simpler than has hitherto been the case in Canada. One of the most significant factors in indigenously creating the British and American nationalities was a single "action-response" mechanism: late feudal England disassociated itself from Christian concepts of Universal Brotherhood and stressed local (ie national) interests based, to a large degree, on materialistic considerations; similarly, the Thirteen Colonies united against a much broader Imperial organization in defence of local (again, national) material interests.

But the Anglo-American national definition was relatively simple because the identification of friend and foe presented no problem. Canada's situation has been complicated by the very impossibility of a singular action-response mechanism which defines clearly an indigenous nationalism in response to a *singular* extraterritorialism. The two major schools of historical thought have been themselves indicative of the non-national dilemma. In being "trapped" between the European-British connection and the United States in associating Canadian interests — strategic, defence, constitutional, political, economic — with one or the other power, a totally indigenous Canadian orientated psychology has been impossible. But that, of course, has been changing because the historical problem of Canada facing two attractive metropoles has passed away.

More than a decade ago George Grant lamented the passing of Canadian nationalism in the face of the growing imperial American menace. What was dying away, of course, was the traditional Canadian empathy and sense of association with Great Britain. Grant moves down familiar paths of criticism long established by the conservative-liberal school by accusing the Liberal Party in aiding and abetting the Americanization process after 1940. What provoked Grant's now-famous lament,[4] and, for him, signified the collapse of Canadian empathy for Britain and the countervailing supremacy of American influence was the somewhat brutal ousting of Conservative Prime Minister John G Diefenbaker in the early 1960s by Canadians largely unconscious of the (Americanizing) significance of their gesture. Since the United States has been a vast engine of liberalism, the only logical Canadian rebuttal, proclaims Grant, should come in a socialist guise, utilizing the full force of the state to halt the various aspects of Americanism.

For Grant, the great betrayers of Canada have been the capitalistic interests, a group which consistently lacks any sense of Canadian loyalty. But capitalism need not always be disloyal, as Grant seems to believe; that has been a specific problem confronting Canadian capitalism which has never been associated with an indigenous liberal sense of Canadian nationality. Nor will socialism solve the problem of a lesser country sharing a continent with a liberal superpower. Canada socialized, one suspects, would still be a relatively static society facing a highly dynamic one, with a socialist Canada remaining no less vulnerable by the continued necessity of importing its technology. That alone would maintain Canada in a state of colonial dependence. Indeed, Grant himself recognized that Canadians have attempted a ridiculously impossible task in trying to build a "conservative nation" (Grant's terminology) in the age of progress. But nations of the Anglo-American type have been, by definition, non-conservative, progressive, liberal, devoted to modernity. The real Canadian failure is that Canadians never tried to create a genuine (ie independent or "localistic" and liberal) nation state because of their ingrained empathy for the Imperial connection. Ideologically speaking, Canada remains a throwback to the pre-national period.

V

There are two usual methods of defining traditional ideological "Canadianism". One is to examine it in terms of Canadian historical development. Another is to examine Canadianism in terms of the Anglo-American world and, by logical extension, in terms of Western Civilization. Within the context of Canadian development, one finds in the first instance a point long recognized by the conservative liberal school of historians; namely, that Canada was strictly a political-economic (as opposed to a popular ideological) concept. The country was organized economically, politically, and constitutionally around the extractive mechanisms of the east-west staples trade from the seventeenth to the early twentieth century. Also within the context of Canadian development — but from the viewpoint of the liberal school — grew the concept of Canada as an ideological extension, but not a political or constitutional extension, of the United States. But the fact remains that in both traditional liberalistic schools of thought the integration of ideology with politics and economics has been lacking.

The socio-ideological fragmentation of Canadian society has also been recognized at the more obvious level of politics. The Liberals and the Conservatives reflected the differing views of the national Canadian identity, one favouring the (North) American tradition, the other the European tradition. But surely no country can have two nationalisms. Such would indicate that the country was not, by definition, a nation, precisely because either the necessary integrating mechanism has not worked or has never existed. What some commentators have served up is merely political rhetoric in the guise of a discussion of nationalism and, in so doing, have failed to grapple adequately with the lack of a truly Canadian nationalism. Instead of Canadian political parties operating in the same ideological system as in the United States, the parties themselves represent different ideologies. Consequently, while both major Canadian parties aspire to be "national", neither has been nor can be successful in that regard.

Both the Liberal Party and the Conservative Party have been married to exclusive interests with vague ethnic overtones, the Liberals to the "French", the Conservatives to the "English". But neither of these exclusive interests, in turn, has exhibited any especially Canadian empathy: indeed, even in Quebec, the home of the original term "Canadian" which once conveyed a sense of distinction *vis-à-vis* the French before 1760 and the English afterwards, the term as an instrument of identity has been retreating before the more localistic *Québécois*. Although Canada has never been a strong ideological concept, this is, nonetheless, a noteworthy measure of Canadian decline, and, if it appears more advanced in Quebec than elsewhere, it has been so because the French-speaking population there has been more blatantly limited and exclusive in attitude longer than the rest of the country.

The central crisis of Canada — and, indeed, of the Liberals and Conservatives as Parties — has been the failure to liberalize, to create a common value system whose very *raison d'être* is equated to the very existence of Canada without reference to exclusive, limited community interests of ethnicity, class, provincialism and/or regionalism. The recent attempts by the federal government to encourage bilingualism and multiculturalism, especially the former, as a means of pacifying the discontent of various communities in Canada has been hopelessly futile because these gestures have contained no especially Canadian quality. Any linguistic emphasis *de facto* denies a distinct Canadian quality and automatically provokes internal disunity. The increasingly popular theory which has sought to engender a sense of popular Canadianism grounded in social and ideological diversity leads to an impossible *cul de sac*. And yet the federal government's policy, it must be conceded, has been totally consistent with the widely held and accepted view of Canada as a mosaic. In keeping with the traditional pluralistic or mosaic ideology, Canadianism constitutes a recognition and acceptance of a multitude of ideologies and/or philosophies among its constituent population, ideologies and/or philosophies which may, themselves, be far more attractive and command more loyalty from their adherents than Canada, itself.

The other aspect of the examination of Canadianism, with specific reference to the Anglo-American world, is now in order. National concepts in the Anglo-American world have not only been a matter of the integration of politics, constitutionalism, economics and geography, but also have involved a popular ideological commitment to distinct, identifiable values. Because of the essential integration and association of basic concepts, one can use such terms as Americanism, nationalism, and liberalism, if not interchangeably, then at least in the certainty that these have been extensions of a commonly-held value system. Extreme liberal values have been basic to that quality which has historically denoted the United States *vis-à-vis* the rest of the world. Consequently, when one speaks of American nationalism or Americanism, one is, *de facto*, referring to liberalism — or, more precisely, that variant of liberalism that came to maturity in (North) America. Similarly, when one speaks of the British nationality — especially in the previous century since it has weakened recently under the impact of socialism/toryism and local ethnic revival — one refers to the liberal variant which matured in the British Isles and which was somewhat weaker or more conservative than the (North) American strain.

Liberalism has been the more general or more universal concept and nationalism its more specific and limited application geographically, constitutionally, and politically. Nothing comparable has occurred in Canada, where the logical singularity of liberalism retreated before pluralism. The concept of being Canadian or of Canadianism has consequently been far more nebulous than liberal nationalism. Liberal American nationalism has been an integrated concept involving ideology, politics, and economics, whereas Canadianism has been a constitutional, political, and economic concept only. For this reason, Canadianism and Americanism have not been analogous concepts. By logical extension of the foregoing, moreover, since internal distinction has been fundamental to the Canadian ideology and constitution, the promotion of extreme provincialism and ethnicity which threatens the country's existence is also consistent with its ideology. In this way the Canadian ideology is potentially anti-Canadian and one might use, instead of Canadianism, the term (anti-)Canadianism to identify the inherent and somewhat paradoxical contradiction in the ideology itself as a self-negating force.

If the British and Americans equated their nationalism to liberalism, then traditional (anti-)Canadianism was conceptually defined, *de facto,* to the right of the Anglo-American world. No doubt the consistent Canadian tradition of defeat and inhibition had much to do with this. The extraterritorial influence of France and Great Britain had downgraded local initiatives in religion, commerce, politics. The Conquest, the revolutionary American invasion of 1775, the War of 1812, the Rebellions of 1837, even the Confederation of 1867 — all were associated with the British political tradition and each constituted a rejection of things American. In so rejecting Americanism, the Canadians as a matter of fact had also rejected functional liberalism and thus, unwittingly, the entire Anglo-American tradition. But, if it is apparent that Canada was defined to the conceptual right of the Anglo-American world, then the extent or degree of that rightward position is not so easily discerned. All one can state with any certainty is that if Canadianism has been to the right of various brands of national liberalism — American, British, French — then Canadianism has been to the left of *unqualified* ethnic, class and provincial/regional tendencies. Otherwise, Canada would never have existed in any form.

In other words, although pluralistic and non-homogeneous, there have been sufficient forces at work (historically the political-economy of the east-west staples trade) to overcome a total breakdown of Canada. But further to the right the fragmenting tendencies — rampant ethnicity, the transformation of classes into fullblown estates, and provincialism/regionalism — are becoming more pervasive. It is this tradition of rightward predominance which has become stronger in the seventh decade of this century. Since the decline of the staples system and with no other *raison d'être,* the fragmentation of Canada has become ever more imminent and to be a Canadian with one's recognition of the validity of pluralism, is, in effect, to accept the ultimate rationale of that pluralism — the destruction of the country. Moving rightward, the various inconsistencies of class-estatism, provincialism, regionalism, and ethnicity become so intense that the previous political-constitutional groupings break down as new societies appear. Such occurred in Austria-Hungary and the Ottoman Empire, almost shattered Russia (1917-1921) and, of course, now threaten Canada. Teetering between the examples of Anglo-American liberalism on the left and intensifying exclusive interests on the right, one can only guess at the outcome for Canada. Like France in the 1780s, Canada is rapidly approaching a point of socio-ideological decision. And like Versailles in the 1780s, the central authority in Ottawa appears singularly unable to deal with the fragmenting tendencies.

Regarding the role of Ottawa, three points may be made. First, in the broadest terms Ottawa's basic obligation has been to provide for "peace, order and good government" from which one might logically extrapolate an obligation to defend the interests of its citizens. But even that function has been doubtful, because Ottawa was not created as the result of the liberal quest for state power to defend private property and civil rights. The central government's moral authority is in an advanced state of decay precisely because Canadians, in looking toward the Anglo-American world as a model for Canada, have expected Ottawa to function similarly to the Anglo-American authorities — a function for which Ottawa was never constitutionally equipped. The traditional basic function of the state in Canada, in accord with the staples economy, has been to import technologies and to use them to organize the continental interior and also, in accord with pluralism, to mediate between varied competing interests. The first obligation of continental organization has long been accomplished and the second, with the persistent demands of exclusive economic and ethnic interests and with ten provinces reflecting an infinity of special situations, is too complex for the present constitutional structure which did, after all, start with only four provinces.

Secondly, Ottawa is less the arbiter of powerful interests than it once was because the Judicial Committee and the provinces have reduced its legal authority. The disintegrating tendencies of (anti-)Canadianism are everywhere prevalent and Ottawa is helpless to stem the tide precisely because it is part of the tide. Once the most essential part of the old order in terms of engineering the staples extractive mechanisms, Ottawa has become the most super-fluous aspect.

Thirdly, in the study of Canadian history one cannot but note that much has been made of Canada's colonial legacy and status, of its subordination and deference to extraterritorial authority. What has consistently been neglected in this perspective has been the fact that Canada, itself, has really been almost an Imperial structure — a replica, if you will, of its French and British predecessors. The *ancien regime* of France had been devoted to diversity and the British government after the American Revolution never seriously attempted to homogenize its colonial holdings so long as apparent stability prevailed. Even the attempt to alter the ideology of Lower Canada after 1840 was quite brief. Ottawa seems to have inherited the traditional Imperial attitude of a grudging and distant tolerance so long as peace and order charac-terized the provincial dependencies, a fact aided, no doubt, by the country's size and diverse geography. For these reasons, Ottawa cannot possibly focalize and muster rising popular Canadianism to offset the Quebec secessionists or belligerent Westerners who are, themselves, simply the logical result of the (anti-)Canadian old order. Indeed, when the representatives and leaders of the Ottawa-branch of the old order, irrespective of their political persuasion — Liberal, Conservative, New Democrat — claim that they will not lead the country into a civil war, they are probably correct. The *raison d'être* of the old order, the east-west trade in staples, has gone and with it went the unifying imperative and the will to sustain Confederation Canada.

VI

Aside from the imponderable dilemma of a precise definition of Canada's position on the socio-ideological model, what has made the model so attractive for this inquiry in relation to various aspects of European history is that it permits the investigator to recognize (historical?) evolution within a totally illiberal framework. This is of enormous significance for the study of Canadian history because all too often the evolving crisis has been regarded as a conflict between the left and right *only* with the alleged forces of the left and right improperly identified because of the fundamental inadequacy of the liberal and Marxist frameworks in evaluating societies outside the Anglo-American tradition. The federal-provincial/regional conflict, the ethnic/linguistic/multicultural issue, the problem of exclusive class/estatism have all been problems within the context of the illiberal right insofar as Canadian history is concerned and thereby it differs markedly from Anglo-American and pre-twentieth century west European history. Traditional liberalistic concepts of left and right mean nothing in Canada because they have no relation to power shifts of a non-popular nature involving only exclusive, limited interests. Such power transference from a central government to provinces or regions, from one ethnic group to another, from one class or estate to another bears no relation to reform or to reaction: liberalistic conceptual terminology simply does not apply.

By way of conclusion, one may say that Canada has been twice removed from a national existence: Canada has clearly not been an Anglo-American type of nation state because it never liberalized; aside from this observation, however, non-national Canada is in deep difficulty, because no legitimized sense of common Canadianism exists, even outside a liberal context. Most rightward tending societies have a single distinctive ethnic and linguistic foundation which has been associated with the *raison d'être* of the community. Not even that has existed in Canada as a binding force. On the right has been traditional (anti-)Canadianism translating potentially and variously into pseudo-ethnicities, into the provinces as new "nationalities", or into continental integration or, at an earlier time, into the proposed British Imperial federation. The point is simply this: the Canadian conceptual framework has been multi-dimensional and infinitely more complex than most appear to have realized. This complexity has gone unrecognized because the liberal and conservative liberal historians and, more recently, the Marxists have not adequately ascertained the significance of pluralism in Canada. Canadian society is disintegrating because its constituent blocs no longer communicate within the same conceptual framework. Such is the crisis of the old order in Canada by which is simply meant the sum totality of all significant traditional relationships presently in a process of collapse. (Anti-)Canadianism is denying the very validity of the country's existence, even as an illiberal structure.

VII

Aside from the crisis within the context of the right, there has been another aspect to the crisis of Canada, a crisis of liberalism. Somewhat like France before the Revolution and quite distinct from rightward traditional (anti-)Canadianism has arisen a new, popular (more truly liberal) Canadianism. Popular Canadianism has arisen against a unique background, the end of liberal universality in the United States and the corresponding transformation of the latter into a nation state. The pre-twentieth century Canadian past has been a record of the rejection of universality and, indeed, it would not be a distortion to claim that Canada was virtually the universal American antithesis. By its very nature, the *uni*versal concept of liberal America did not permit another comparable social structure; to have liberalized, Canada would have necessarily Americanized in every conceivable sense and, in effect, would have ceased being a distinct structure. When America lost its universality, the profoundly antithetical quality in Canadian-American relations eroded. The *necessarily* illiberal dimension of Canadian evolution has been ending. Paradoxically, Canada has been finding its liberal dimension developing just as that ideology has been losing its functional vitality elsewhere. But for Canada the liberalizing process has been evolving within an illiberal system and its popularity has, consequently, not been marked by legal and/or constitutional recognition.

According to Kari Levitt, the new mercantilism of direct investment in Canada by multinational corporations, most of whose head offices are located in the United States, has acted as a transmission belt of new values. Discussing the economic concepts associated with continentalism, Levitt has discounted them as valid theories for a viable Canadian existence. The result of continentalist economic thinking has been to elevate Canada to the status of the world's richest underdeveloped country.[5] A significant factor in Canada's status has been the "technology gap", wherein occurs little indigenous technological adaptation and innovation, a colonial monetary system, *de facto* subservience to extraterritorial law, and the seeking of concessions from other lands (especially the United States) which can be easily and arbitrarily revoked. The crucial factor in this process, according to Levitt, has been the replication of American society. The new American multinational industrial system has been so structured as to encourage the productive side of the economy to dictate wants to the consumer and to influence his values, thereby determining supplies, technology, capital goods, and distribution. Because the corporation has been sovereign in its planning and the consumer has been captivated by the attractive living standards of the metropole, the tendency has been to homogenize countries like Canada which interact extensively with the United States. Common values have obviously been desirable from the corporate viewpoint because they lead to similar products, high production efficiencies and profits.

The international corporation, Levitt assures us, has declared war on the nation state (including Canada, of course, in Levitt's view), with its local democratic decision-making authority eroded before the onslaught of internationalism, modernization, and materialism. Working to some degree off the views of George Grant, Levitt has accepted the proposition that the Canadian ruling class has exchanged its "nationalism" for profit; that is to say, it has joined the continentalist thrust because it can profit more as a managerial class for the international American corporations than as an indigenous entrepreneurial class. So long as Britain was a significant factor in Canada and the monarchy commanded the loyalty of the ruling class, the anti-American axis of English-Canadian business and the French-Canadian clerical elite had held firm. With the British Imperial demise, the sense of destiny and stewardship of the traditional elites was lost. Operating through the Liberal Party, the predominant class sold out the country to American interests which, unlike earlier British investments, were based on equity. The north-south restructuring has tended to undermine Ottawa and thus its ability to redistribute wealth which, in turn, has encouraged the provinces to invite foreign investment. This has, claims Levitt, hastened the Americanization process. In Levitt's *schema* (like that of Creighton and other staples theorists), American continentalism has destroyed the old (east-west) tie and has integrated the economic and cultural life of Canada into a new (American continental) reality. The resulting coincidence of Canadian-American interest has tended to foster, according to Levitt, a coincidence of the policies of the political leaderships in both countries, a fact which has eroded Canadian independence, even if its formality remains indefinitely.

In framing her thesis, Levitt makes several significant points. First, she notes that national communities have been under attack from the homogenizing effects of the multinationals. But Canada has never been a genuine nation state and that fact, not the evident vigour of the multinationals, has been the central problem. By its very nature, Canada's pluralism has rendered the country quite willing to absorb and to experiment with ever new values. The United States has been an integrated society — ideologically, politically, economically — and it is only logical that, given favourable circumstances, the popular American economy would follow its market northward with all the attendant ideological consequences for Canada. And the Canadian self-perception aided the American economic takeover. Traditional (anti-)Canadianism was exclusive and not popular because of the ethnic dimension and because the country's political-economy was a by-product of the old exclusive east-west staples trade. Consequently, pluralistic traditional (anti-)Canadianism never prepared the populace to resist popular (foreign) economic control. That control has flowed from the Canadian predisposition, since the seventeenth century, to import technologies from Europe and, more recently, from the United States either in finished or in blueprint form. The creation of technologies has been associated with the imperative of environmental mastery and with the inclination to innovate, in turn related to the ideological left with its anti-feudal progressive and universal sense. Having created a society out of a virgin continent like the Americans, the Canadians have been no less willing to utilize technology, but, unlike the United States, Canada has been less committed to a total reworking of the tangible environment and the rightward Canadian outlook has never been so orientated to necessary progress. In addition, technological involvement in Canada via the original east-west exclusivist trade in staples had dictated a limited, rather than popular, Canadian commitment to indigenous technological development.

The Canadian mentality, as opposed to the American, has always been concerned with less materialistic, less tangible, less concrete issues. That has been why major issues in Canada have often involved the conservative symbols of ethnicity, race, religion, and language. Traditional (anti-)Canadianism was simply too adaptive, too flexible, and too nebulous to deal with the popular American intrusion. That American liberalism, moreover, has been monolithic and relatively uncompromising has made Canadian ideological "softness" fair game. When liberalism in the guise of the Americanization process initially tried to enter Canada in 1775, 1812, and 1837, it was defeated by persistent rightward shifts. The present difference is, of course, that such obvious rightward pressure is inconsistent with Canada's economic well-being because interdependence with the United States has become so all-pervasive. Nor has this process being limited to any especial group or part of Canada. Levitt concludes her study with a noteworthy suggestion: "Only the emergence of a new value system within English Canada can insure the continued existence of a nation here."[6] The solution is quite obvious: the very process which Levitt decries *is* the new value system — new to Canada, that is.

The Americanization process has involved in Canada, not a singular process, but two processes — each with ideological effects at opposite ends of the socio-ideological spectrum. On the right has been the regional-continentalism that Levitt rightly fears: the new north-south staples axis, the strengthening of the provinces, the erosion of Ottawa's authority as the symbol of the old (east-west) trade in staples. The physical mechanisms by which the new mercantile system works — especially the communication and transportation systems — are destructive to the traditional Canadian existence. So too is the continental corporate structure which includes international unions. It is this dimension that staples theorists — Creighton, Innis, Naylor — have criticized. But then one must also remember that traditional Canada was a relatively simple structure of political-economy designed mostly for staples extraction and the political accommodation of various diverse interests. As such, Canada absorbed the Imperial commitment to blind anti-Americanism and anti-populism which suited both the staples elite and the Bleu pluralists. Ideologically illiberal, Canada had *already* stabilized to the potentially disintegrating and negating right when the north-south trading mechanisms encouraging regional-continentalism started to interact.

On the other hand, quite aside from the traditional structures of the Canadian political economy and its pluralistic ideology, American-inspired liberalism itself has started to expand the Canadian socio-ideological spectrum leftward. Liberalism has arrived in the form of attitudes, philosophy, and ideology expressed via the personnel of the corporate system and of its efficient replication outside America. When Levitt noted the danger of Americanization to Ottawa, she was only partly correct. The new American inspired liberalism is a danger to the *entire* traditional Canadian order as represented by the constitutional structure of 1867, federal *and* provincial. In assessing French Canada's reluctance to be drawn, along with the rest of the country, into the American empire, Levitt has suggested recognition of a special status for Quebec. This is an interesting position because it indicates that Levitt has been thinking along fairly traditional lines of pluralism and (anti-)Canadianism and is flirting with potential disintegration as a solution to the crisis of Confederation. Extreme provincialism and separatism are fundamentally in the ideological mainstream of the 1867 constitution with its *de facto* pluralism. Indeed, what both decentralizers and centralizers working within the 1867 context do not seem to comprehend is that their respective positions only represent different sides of the same issue. And a false issue, at that. The real problem has been developing outside the 1867 context. Unnoticed by the old order has been the fact that the country has been liberalizing.

The very value transmission which Levitt has decried has been inundating Canada constantly from the American metropolis. If the mechanisms of the neo-staples trade tend to draw Canada, by regional affiliation, into a continental economic system, then the ideas, beliefs, sentiments and values arriving from the United States stress traditional liberal monolithism. In other words, although Canadians are being "Americanized" by virtue of a common value system, that value system still retains elements of traditional liberal individualism, entrepreneurialism, and respect for innovation. And in Canada, the *political* translation of this independent attitude so vitally new to Canadians need not lead to continental integration. There is no reason why the politics of American-inspired liberalism in Canada will not be Canadian. After all, the past two decades when the alleged Americanization process has been most intense has generated the most pronounced sense of (anti-American) Canadian nationalism. Insofar as liberalism has been associated with this nationalism, it probably has been genuine nationalism of the Anglo-American type. For Canada, as previously noted, the elimination of the "two metropole" system, generally, and of Great Britain, specifically, has not been a curse, as Grant and Creighton believe, but has rather been a godsend permitting for the first time establishment of an "action-reaction" mechanism involving the United States. Conceivably, this could open the way for a Canadian gesture of independence like the English Act of Supremacy in 1534 and the American Declaration in 1776. Out of the ancient division and confusion regarding Canadian loyalties to the British ideal or the American may yet arise a singular self-seeking Canadian imperative. Uncluttered by pseudo-"British" considerations, the new popular Canadianism may now coalesce into a homogeneous and logically consistent indigenous force sufficient to offset the American monolith. If Creighton has been correct in evaluating Britain as a necessary counterweight to the United States, he may only have been correct to the degree that non-national and pluralistic Canada required such assistance.

Liberalism has always been international, but the transmission of its values need not necessarily lead to integration with the United States as Levitt fears. On the contrary, liberalism has tended to engender highly dynamic socio-political structures well able to defend their own (self-seeking) interests. When Levitt indicated that the American metropole transformed the hinterland into a replica which meant its destruction and disintegration, she missed the point: that replication is a total process *including the ability to adapt liberalism to indigenous politics.* In receiving liberalism, Canada is also obtaining the ideological will to resist its continental implications.

Traditional Canada had not been as Innis, Creighton and the staples theorists would claim, a product of Europe or, more properly, has been so only in a highly qualified sense of having replicated pre-(liberal) revolutionary western Europe. Nor has Canada been merely a northern extension of the United States by virtue of similar environmentally conditioning circumstances or by virtue of attempts to emulate, by a slower process, its British decolonization. Traditional Canada had experienced a contrary ideological evolution which had rejected the integrating liberalism of western Europe and of the Anglo-American world. While the latter, admittedly, has been moving back toward pluralism, the significant fact is that pluralism only reappeared *after* a liberal period. Canada has remained pre-liberal because a popular economy has never definitively dictated its ideology. The latter is manifested as illiberal pluralism which meshed first with the staples system and, subsequently, with branch-plant extra-territorialism, the economic situation being neither an extension of the ideology nor a threat to it. Accordingly, the American threat, in any immediate sense, is incidental rather than fundamental because its economic domination of Canada is not immediately imperilling Canadian ideological pluralism. Indeed, one may even argue that by strengthening liberal proclivities, Americanism is broadening the Canadian value system. But paradoxically in so doing, the seeds of liberalism are just now taking root within the framework of a late-blooming feudal state and also within the context of an age which has been running strongly in an illiberal direction. It is ironic that in the liberalizing period Canada adhered to a pre-liberal ideology and that, in the post-liberal age, Canada seems more popularly liberal.

VIII

Popular Canadianism must not be confused with traditional pluralistic (anti-)Canadianism with which it shares geography. (Anti-)Canadianism was of feudal inspiration and derivation; popular Canadianism has been of liberal inspiration. The old order in Canada has long been associated with traditional (anti-)Canadianism with its fragmenting political-constitutional institutions and its classes and ethnicities divided against themselves. The new popular Canadianism has no distinct indigenous mechanisms for self-expression and that is central to the crisis although never really articulated because of the rhetorical smoke-screen cast up by the ongoing controversy within the right. Nonetheless, the Americanization of Canada — its essential liberalization — has conjured up genuine socio-ideological problems and presented distinct alternatives which have gone unaddressed for too long. One must not assume, however, as the issue is resolved, that liberalism will win out over rampant pluralism as it did elsewhere in the West. It is altogether conceivable that Canada may be the first Western land to turn away consciously from the age of progress. Should that occur, Canada must not expect to survive for long, having given full rein to its disintegrating and self-negating ideology.

Conclusion

I

The Anglo-American world evolved along a singular direction from the tenth until the nineteenth century. One must not make similar assumptions about a comparable evolutionary type in illiberal societies. In illiberal societies, conflict and shifts in power tend to occur within the rightward context, rather than negating that context. Thus, the collisions between estates or limited communities in their varied forms generally involve no left-right results. Because such societies permit diverse values, innumerable regulations and bureaucratic mechanisms have been needed to service them: the internal dynamic has been devoted to balance not progress. What is most disconcerting about the right has been its conceptual divorcement, the breakdown of communication within a society of differing interests who may even speak the same ethnic language but not the same ideological one. Hence, the necessity of regulation and guidance from above. As in medieval feudalism, such a society arms against itself as against the outsider.

Canada was definitionally the virtual antithesis of the Anglo-American left with its explicit egalitarian universality. Two distinct exclusive traditions meshed in the creation of Canada: Bleu corporatism associated with the political economy of the east-west trade in staples. The latter, until this century, had always outweighed the fragmenting pluralism of the former whose advent has coincided with the new north-south regional-continental economic reality. Because Canada has never been a monolithic society with the total popular integration of its ideology, politics, and economics, Canada has been, conceptually, to the right of the Anglo-American world. The triumph of the Bleu legacy in the 1896 election has predisposed the country to an unrestricted rightward drift and, in effect, to its own ultimate negation.

Pluralism in Canada has been regarded as an act of social justice and as the basis of a rather colourful social mosaic, all of which tends to obscure its more negative qualities as the author of various injustices. From pluralism and community interests of a limited type derive the inflexibility of federal politics; from pluralism derives the enclaves of economic and corporate power where certain (ethnic) interests are well entrenched; and, associated with the last point, from pluralism derives the failure of vertical mobility in Canada, the country having never been committed to careers open to talent. From pluralism, too, derives the regional/provincial emphasis, the disintegrating state structure, the ominous sense of drift associated with no overriding imperative.

Despite the liberal fragment emanating from the United States, the existing reality of Canada precludes creating a society as truly liberal as the Anglo-American world in its formative period. But Canadian inspiration could be drawn from the left. Most Canadians, after all, do tend to favour liberal egalitarianism in law and politics. Probably, it would be advisable to enshrine these benefits, constitutionally, just as it would be equally advisable to curb the excesses of the self-seeking imperial provinces in support of common Canadian interests. So too with foreign economic domination — a truly national sense is imperative to limit its excesses. Just as Jeffersonianism nationalized English liberalism two centuries ago, so may the Canadianization of the liberal fragment emanating from the United States be both the solution to the most salient internal problems and the logical instrument of definitive decolonization. Traditional Canadian definitional anti-liberalism had involved a *total* rejection of "things American" — political, economic, *and* ideological. But one must remember that the anti-papal gestures of late medieval England were constitutional, political, and economic, not ideological. Initially, the dispute did not involve Catholicism and fundamental beliefs. Similarly the anti-British gestures of the revolutionary United States were not ideological, for Americans retained — and exaggerated — the liberal ideology. Based on historical precedent, it would appear quite possible for Canada to absorb the liberal fragment without submission to the continental imperative.

II

Marxism and socialism have been the theoretical extensions of functional liberalism. To Marxism went the liberalistic concept of linear history and progress which was defined as further to the left of functional liberalism. With this notion of a far left came a stronger, more blatant statement of universality involving ultimate global adherence to Marxism. The liberals stressed the political and legal aspects of egalitarianism; the Marxists stressed the economic and social aspects. Just as liberalism had rejected the legal and political exclusivity of the feudal system, so did Marxism attempt to shift the partial achievement of liberalism to its (emancipatory) result by removing the political and legal dimension which rested on propertied individualism. In fact, Marxism inadvertently associated itself with resurgent feudalism. Marxism had wished to enrol the industrialization process in its attempted mastery of the environment as much as the liberals did; in so doing, Marxism automatically rendered itself a parochial "class" philosophy which denied its pretence to universality and associated it with concepts derived from the medieval social order. Because Marxism was theoretical, not functional, it has been prone to redefinition according to various parochial necessities — Leninism, Maoism, Castroism, and so forth. Despite its emphasis on history, Marxism provided even less an impartial basis for historical inquiry than has liberalism which assumed a somewhat random evolutionary quality in human affairs; Marxism was decidedly eschatological and collapsed liberal empiricism based on random change into an indistinguishable unity of perceiver and object, both influenced by the ubiquitous "forces of production".

III

The neo-feudalism of the (post-)industrial world is far more complex than that of medieval feudalism, largely because of industry and technology. Liberalism was essentially a pre-industrial ideology which just happened to forward the industrial genesis by virtue of its entrepreneurial psychology and its free market economics. But it would be unwise to place anything more than a casual and temporary emphasis on the liberal-industrial nexus. Industry *was* sparked by the liberalistic attitude but industrial maturity did not accord with egalitarianism. True, industry has become more popular and has drawn most Western peoples into an industrial-urban environment. But industry and urban life have also fractured society into innumerable overlapping groupings in a most non-liberal fashion. While industry may impose an overriding outlook and perspective on life, as some claim, by the very nature of its products in the marketplace creating common global wants, increasing specialization in the workplace has had the contrary effect of fracturing society. The structures of government and business are, moreover, also becoming quite rigid. Mobility still exists for the technically and professionally competent but everywhere occurs a new entrenchment, a new infinity of rules and regulations which are undoing the unique achievement of Western revolutionary emancipation. Rightward societies, given their inherent irrationality, are well able to accommodate the integrated global marketplace and the fragmented workplace. The new feudalism promises not to be class orientated in the Marxist sense because its variety is virtually unlimited.

IV

Socio-ideological evolution has been more complex than historically linear liberal and Marxist/socialistic theory permits. History has not been necessarily linear, uni-directional, integrating but has been limited to empirical superficiality. By stressing the perceptible aspects of race, ethnicity, culture, language, religion, the empirical *aspect* of liberalism provided the parochial societies in the nineteenth and twentieth centuries with explicit encouragement for division of the human community along lines casually termed "national"; this was a paradoxical reversal of the fundamental egalitarian universality on which cosmopolitan liberalism rested. The superficial adoption of the benefits of a matured liberalism by parochial/ethnic and historically peripheral societies such as Canada or eastern and central Europe has tended to deceive those who have attempted to replicate liberalism. The adoption of liberal language, concepts, political ideas and economic theory and the utilization (not creation) of liberal-inspired advanced technology by parochial, "non-historical" peoples has created high but unjustified expectations for betterment through progress. Such confusion relates directly to historical theory which, with its ingrained liberal roots, has assumed the monolithic value-integration of all societies after the liberal fashion. This has been a false assumption. In most societies — certainly where Western technology, political and economic concepts have been imparted over the relatively short time of a century or two — the traditional values linger, especially when no great act of public violence burned away competing systems.

V

History, the discipline, has never been as autonomous or as independent as the ideals which it has expounded. The classical liberal departure cut Western man away from his familiar corporate values and historical study was, at least partly, a response to this departure, an attempt to impose a sense of certainty. Historical study rationalized the new order and justified the denial of the old one; in so doing, historical study was not an entirely dispassionate advocate but rather a subtle propaganda instrument. History as a discipline helped legitimize the new and unfamiliar stress on propertied individualism. But history has only been an aspect of culture and, to that degree, has been as limited as the parochial cultures whose quick demise it, without warrant, had assumed only a few short decades ago. But the parochial cultures have strengthened and (liberal) history has weakened, a discipline in search of a purpose — an impossibility in the (neo-)feudal world. History was the unique creation of right to left evolution. Change may, of course, occur specifically within a rightward context, but because of *ideological* fixity, that was not historical change. The monolithic quality of the liberal left also had a deadening effect on historical inquiry. An historical notion seems to require both a left and right from whose interacting tension and from whose *ideological* distance has been created that sense of time and space so basic to conceptualization and historical comprehension.

VI

The present century has stood, so to speak, in the shadow of the eighteenth and nineteenth centuries with their liberalistic notions of civil rights and individualism whereas the social and economic imperatives of this century have dictated organizational structures ideologically akin to feudalism. The difficulty has been that people want the best of both worlds: they want individualism, freedom, civil rights; they also want to forego the potential adversities of truly liberal (free market) economics. In Canada, and more recently in the United States, ethnic groups insist on vertical social mobility but also insist on the "rights" of their special interests. The real inhibitor to social mobility has been the ingrained communitarian concept which has insisted on self-replication and has not stressed the (liberalistic) values of social mobility based on merit.

VII

All men are entrapped by the reality of a physical existence. The modern world has offered at least two alternatives by which the materialistic imperatives of humankind may be satisfied through the mastery of nature: (classical) liberalism with its harnessing of the worst aspects of human nature, and Marxism/socialism with its attempt to curb the appetites accepted by liberalism. It would seem that the vast majority of mankind, even in the liberal heartland, is turning away from the left. What remains of liberalism, if one may presume to emphasize a somewhat Platonic dimension, is the very concept of liberalism as a functional and historical reality. The concept of an anti-feudal left has been fixed as a viable (unlike pretentious Marxism) alternative to functional feudalism both medieval and new, both European/Canadian and corporate-liberal American. The liberal reality has actually occurred and achieved its place as a genuine historical and ideological concept; it cannot be disproved, as can Marxism, which was conceptually brilliant but which failed the test of historical reality. Marxism never contributed to the *functional* definition of the socio-ideological spectrum.

VIII

Both Marxism and liberalism have claimed to represent an ultimate world-historical terminus[1] with its associated universality, but, by definition, only one ideology may be truly (functionally) universal. From their nineteenth century position, the Marxists looked back to the liberalistic departure which they incorrectly perceived as an ongoing aspect of the feudal to liberal evolution with an inevitable socialistic terminus in an equally predictable future. Unfortunately, Marxism blatantly attached itself to the new limited industrialism and to rightward class-proletarian parochialism; the world-historical terminus to which Marxism aspired had actually been previously achieved by American classical liberalism. The classical liberal left was fixed and had no fluidity, unlike the right. Within the right, social and political relationships, based on corporate groupings, altered and recombined into new relationships. Nothing comparable attended the liberal left because such was not possible in an atomistic society with a singular, weak regulatory mechanism, the state. Society could not evolve within the left; the left collapsed theory and practice or function into a singular monolithic unity; to evolve ideologically and to remain liberal was impossible. Society could only evolve toward the right, that is to say, toward the creation of (competing, organized, hierarchical) power structures which, by their nature, commenced the demise of randomly dynamic liberal individualism.

By the same token, the concept of "mature" (non-classical) liberalism with its emphasis on special interests was simply not possible, for these represent illiberal elements arising within and eroding foundational liberalism. Liberalism — as a *functional* reality — *was* classical liberalism, and all other variations merely started that process which denied its existence. In indicating the socio-ideological structure thus " $\angle$ ", one is describing the actual world-historical terminus on the left which has been associated with social fixity and ideological monolithism and universality, and such indication also recognizes the dwindling possibility, as society moves leftward, of social evolution based on organized, fluid power politics. A "side-stepping" evolutionary fashion such as that characteristic of the corporate and pluralistic right has been quite impossible on the left which had evolved historically and progressively.

IX

Canada confronts the dilemma faced earlier by the Western historical peoples but, in one sense, Canadians are more fortunate than their predecessors who did not have the advantage of examining the competing ideologies in light of the achievement of the world-historical terminus. Canadians have, as a consequence, a clearer vision of the options — each with benefits and faults — than did their predecessors, and a correspondingly greater capacity to structure their future. But the options are not unlimited and must conform to ideological possibilities; one cannot merely fantasize options exclusive of the Western socio-ideological spectrum. It defines the limits of functional realities. Alternatives for Canada exist in the form of a liberal fragment and a late blooming feudalism and, ultimately, in the form of a modern, progressive, historical existence with its distorting intolerance and an uninspiring parochialism with its ingrained sense of limitation.

Notes

Chapter One

[1]George Grant, *Technology and Empire: Perspectives on North America*, Toronto, House of Anansi, 1969; *Lament for a Nation: The Defeat of Canadian Nationalism*, Toronto, McClelland and Stewart Limited, 1971 (1965).

[2]R G Collingwood, *The Idea of History*, Oxford University Press, 1966 (1946), p. 29.

Chapter Two

[1]Harold A Innis, *The Fur Trade in Canada*, Toronto, University of Toronto Press, 1956, (revised edition).

[2]Creighton has been a prolific writer for four decades but his essential thoughts may be found in the following: *Towards the Discovery of Canada: Selected Essays*, Toronto, Macmillan of Canada, 1972; *Canada's First Century 1867-1967*, Macmillan, 1970; *The Empire of the St Lawrence*, Macmillan, 1956.

[3]J M S Careless, "Frontierism, Metropolitanism, and Canadian History," *Approaches to Canadian History, Canadian Historical Readings*, Vol. I, University of Toronto Press, 1967, pp. 63-83.

[4]Maurice Careless, "Metropolitanism and Nationalism", *Nationalism in Canada*, ed. Peter Russell, Toronto, McGraw-Hill Company of Canada Limited, 1966, pp. 271-283.

[5]Arthur R M Lower, *Great Britain's Woodyard: British America and the Timber Trade, 1763-1867*, Montreal, McGill Queen's University Press, 1973, p. 7.

[6]A R M Lower, *This Most Famous Stream: The Liberal Democratic Way of Life*, Toronto, The Ryerson Press, 1954, p. 4.

[7]*Ibid.*, p. 149.

[8]E R Adair, "Anglo-French Rivalry in the Fur Trade during the 18th Century", *Canadian History Before Confederation: Essays and Interpretations*, ed. J M Bumsted, Georgetown, Ontario, Irwin-Dorsey Limited, 1972, pp. 144-164.

[9]Sigmund Diamond, "An Experiment in 'Feudalism'; French Canada in the 17th Century," *Ibid.*, pp. 81-109.

[10]J F Bosher, "Government and Private Interests in New France", *Ibid.*, pp. 111-124.

[11]Jean Hamelin, *Economie et Societe en Nouvelle France*, Les Presses Universitaires Laval, 1960, pp. 133, 134.

[12]Fernand Ouellet, *Histoire Economique et Social du Quebec 1760-1850: Structures et Conjoncture*, Montreal, Fides, 1966, p. 14.

[13]W J Eccles, *Canada Under Louis XIV, 1663-1701*, Toronto, McClelland and Stewart, 1964, p. 251.

[14]W J Eccles, *The Canadian Frontier, 1534-1760*, New York, Holt, Rinehart and Winston, 1969, p. 185.

[15]Cameron Nish, "The Nature, Composition and Functions of the Canadian Bourgeoisie, 1729-1748." Bumsted, *Canadian History*, pp. 126-142.

[16]Guy Fregault, *Canadian Society in the French Regime*, The Canadian Historical Association Booklets, No. 3, 1968, p. 7.

[17]W J Eccles, *France in America*, Toronto, Harper and Row, 1972, p. 50.

[18]Eccles, *The Canadian Frontier*, p. 100.

[19]H A Innis and A R M Lower, ed. *Select Documents in Canadian Economic History 1783-1885*, University of Toronto Press, 1933, vol. II, p. 373.

[20]S F Wise, "Upper Canada and the Conservative Tradition", *Profiles of a Province: Studies in the History of Ontario*, ed. Edith G Firth, Toronto, Ontario Historical Society, 1967, pp. 20-33.

[21]William Kilbourn, *The Firebrand: William Lyon Mackenzie and the Rebellion in Upper Canada*, Toronto, Clarke, Irwin and Company, 1969 (copyright 1956), p. 29.

[22]Gerald M Craig, *Upper Canada: The Formative Years 1784-1841*, Toronto, McClelland and Stewart, 1963, pp. 107-109.

[23]Robert E Saunders, "What Was the Family Compact?" *Historical Essays on Upper Canada*, ed. J K Johnson, Toronto, McClelland and Stewart, 1975, pp. 129-139.

[24]Hugh G J Aitken, "The Family Compact and the Welland Canal Company," *Historical Essays*, pp. 153-170.

[25]Margaret Fairley, ed, *The Selected Writings of William Lyon Mackenzie, 1824-1837*, Toronto, Oxford University Press, 1960, p. 224.

[26]Christopher Armstrong and H V Nelles, "Private Property in Peril: Ontario Businessmen and the Federal System, 1898-1911," *Enterprise and National Development: Essays in Canadian Business and Economic History*, ed. Glenn Porter and Robert Cuff, Toronto, Hakkert, 1973, pp. 20-38.

[27]Gad Horowitz, *Canadian Labour in Politics*, University of Toronto Press, 1968. Chapter One.

[28]The majority of Canada West voters, by 1864, clearly wished reconstitution because they could find no solution to the political impasse through either of their two parties. The Conservatives dared not part with Bleu legislative power; the Grits, even with Rouge support, could never gain unqualified control of the lower house because a Rouge alliance automatically precluded certain types of legislative activity. Two options faced the Grit Reformers. The first involved dissolving the Union to eliminate Bleu power and, thereby, place the John A Macdonald Conservatives at the mercy of the Grit Reformers. A new division of Canada would have reopened the pre-1840 economic and jurisdictional problems concerning access to Upper Canada along the St Lawrence. Dissolving the Union, moreover, for the linguistically English of Lower Canada, meant total and possibly unpleasant Bleu supremacy under responsible government. The second possibility of reconstitution along federal lines offered economic opportunity consistent with the objectives of the Conservative Party, a legal-constitutional structure capable of defending Bleu interests, representation by population for the Reformers and a central government, freed from the shackles of deadlock, able to initiate western expansion.

[29]Frank H Underhill, "Some Reflections on the Liberal Tradition in Canada," *Approaches to Canadian History, Canadian Historical Readings*, vol. 1, University of Toronto Press, 1967, pp. 29-41.

[30]Glenn Porter, "Recent Trends in Canadian Business and Economic History," *Enterprise and National Development*, p. 6.

Chapter Three

[1]David V J Bell, "The Loyalist Tradition in Canada," *Canadian History*, pp. 211-229.

[2]Helen Taft Manning, *The Revolt of French Canada, 1800-1835: A Chapter in the History of the British Commonwealth*, Toronto, The Macmillan Company of Canada Limited, 1962, pp. 25, 26.

[3]Lawrence A H Smith, "*Le Canadien* and the British Constitution, 1806-1810," *Constitutionalism and Nationalism in Lower Canada, Canadian Historical Readings*, vol. 5, University of Toronto Press, 1969, pp. 17-32.

[4]W P M Kennedy, ed., *Statutes, Treaties, and Documents of the Canadian Constitution 1713-1929*, Toronto, Oxford University Press, 1930, Liverpool to Craig, 12 September 1810, p. 236.

[5]R T Naylor, "The Rise and Fall of the Third Commercial Empire of the St Lawrence," *Capitalism and the National Question in Canada*, ed. Gary Teeple, University of Toronto Press, 1972, pp. 1-41.

[6]John Conway, "Politics, Culture and the Writing of Constitutions," *Empire and Nations: Essays in Honour of Frederic H Soward*, ed. Harvey L Dyck and H Peter Krosby, University of Toronto Press, 1969, p. 8.

[7]Alfred Dubuc, "The Decline of Confederation and the New Nationalism," *Nationalism in Canada*, ed. Peter Russell, Toronto, McGraw-Hill Company of Canada Ltd., 1966, pp. 112-132.

[8]Michel Brunet, "The French Canadians' Search for a Fatherland," *Ibid.*, pp. 47-60.

[9]Wallace Clement, *The Canadian Corporate Elite: An Analysis of Economic Power*, Toronto, McClelland and Stewart, 1975.

[10]Douglas Hartle, "How to Cope with New Feudalism," *The Financial Post*, Toronto, 4 December 1976, p. 14.

Chapter Four

[1]Richard B Morris, *The Emerging Nations and the American Revolution*, New York, Harper and Row, 1970, p. 10.

[2]Melvin C Wren, *The Course of Russian History*, New York, The Macmillan Company, 1968, p. 79.

Chapter Five

[1]Hilda Neatby, "French-Canadian Nationalism and the American Revolution," *Canadian History*, pp. 197-209.

[2]Fernand Ouellet, "Le Nationalisme canadien-francais: De ses origines a l'insurrection de 1837," *Constitutionalism and Nationalism in Lower Canada, Canadian Historical Readings*, vol. 5, University of Toronto Press, 1969, p. 4.

[3]Adam Shortt, "History of Canadian Metallic Currency", *Money and Banking in Canada: Historical Documents and Commentary*, ed. E P Neufeld, Toronto, McClelland and Stewart Ltd, 1964, p. 120.

[4]George Grant, *Lament for a Nation: The Defeat of Canadian Nationalism*, Toronto, McClelland and Stewart Ltd, 1971.

[5]Kari Levitt, *Silent Surrender: The Multinational Corporation in Canada*, Toronto, Macmillan of Canada, 1970, p. 25.

[6]*Ibid.*, p. 153.

Conclusion

[1]The term "world-historical terminus" is coined advisedly to embody the conceptual predisposition of liberalism to regard itself as the ultimate rendering of humankind in the form of a truly individualistic global society, a notion which has only recently been regarded as fallacious in the face of the resurgence of traditional parochial values. The word "historical" refers to the mechanism — objective, empirical progress in a materialistic sense — by which humankind would walk the path to its final rendition. The anticipated global achievement of a liberalized humanity represented, conceptually, the left, and hence was the *de facto* extremity of socio-ideological evolution. That liberalism was never functionally global in no way detracts from its intent, articulated blatantly by its antithetical materialistic ideology, Marxism. The other dimension or pole of history given its distinctive "side-stepping" evolutionary tendency has no comparable terminal vision. Being parochial, there was no universal or global aspect; being non-progressive or illiberal within a fixed ideological system meant that no fundamental change occurred within the value system — no history existed in the progressivist liberal sense. Non-progressive side-stepping history was truncated in its lack of ideological change. Non-progressive change based on constitutional, political, economic, and often religious flux has been ongoing and, consequently, unlike the world-historical vision of liberalism, has had no ultimate view of the state of humanity.

Selected Bibliography

Approaches to Canadian History. Canadian Historical Readings. University of Toronto Press. Vol. 1 (1967). Vol. 5 (1969).

Bumsted, J M ed. *Canadian History Before Confederation: Essays and Interpretations.* Georgetown, Ontario, Irwin-Dorsey Limited, 1972.

Clement, Wallace. *The Canadian Corporate Elite: An Analysis of Economic Power.* Toronto, McClelland and Stewart, 1975.

Collingwood, R G. *The Idea of History.* Oxford University Press, 1966 (1946).

Craig, Gerald M. *Upper Canada: The Formative Years 1784-1841.* Toronto, McClelland and Stewart, 1963.

Creighton, Donald. *Towards the Discovery of Canada: Selected Essays.* Toronto, Macmillan of Canada, 1972.

_____. *Canada's First Century 1867-1967.* Macmillan, 1970.

_____. *The Empire of the St Lawrence.* Macmillan, 1956.

Dyck, Harvey L. and H Peter Krosby, eds. *Empire and Nations: Essays in Honour of Frederick H Soward.* University of Toronto Press, 1969.

Eccles, W J. *Canada Under Louis XIV, 1663-1701.* Toronto, McClelland and Stewart, 1964.

_____. *The Canadian Frontier, 1534-1760.* New York, Holt, Rinehart and Winston, 1969.

_____. *France in America.* Toronto, Harper and Row, 1972.

Fairley, Margaret, ed. *The Selected Writings of William Lyon Mackenzie, 1824-1837.* Toronto, Oxford University Press, 1960.

Firth, Edith G, ed. *Profiles of a Province: Studies in the History of Ontario.* Toronto, Ontario Historical Society, 1967.

Fregault, Guy. *Canadian Society in the French Regime.* The Canadian Historical Association Booklets, No. 3, 1968.

Grant, George. *Technology and Empire: Perspectives on North America.* Toronto, House of Anansi, 1969.

_____. *Lament For a Nation: The Defeat of Canadian Nationalism.* Toronto, McClelland and Stewart Limited, 1971 (1965).

Hamelin, Jean. *Economie et Societe en Nouvelle France.* Les Presses Universitaires Laval, 1960.

Hartle, Douglas. *The Financial Post.* Toronto, 4 December 1976.

Horowitz, Gad. *Canadian Labour in Politics.* University of Toronto Press, 1968.

Innis, Harold A. *The Fur Trade in Canada.* (Revised edition.) University of Toronto Press, 1956.

Innis H A and A R M Lower, eds. *Select Documents in Canadian Economic History 1783-1885.* University of Toronto Press, 1933, vol. II.

Johnson, J K ed. *Historical Essays on Upper Canada.* Toronto, McClelland and Stewart, 1975.

Kennedy, W P M, ed. *Statutes, Treaties, and Documents of the Canadian Constitution 1713-1929.* Toronto, Oxford University Press, 1930.

Kilbourn, William. *The Firebrand: William Lyon Mackenzie and the Rebellion in Upper Canada.* Toronto, Clarke, Irwin, and Company, 1969. (copyright 1956).

Levitt, Kari. *Silent Surrender: The Multinational Corporation in Canada.* Toronto, Macmillan of Canada, 1970.

Lower, Arthur R M. *Great Britain's Woodyard: British America and the Timber Trade, 1763-1867.* Montreal, McGill Queen's University Press, 1973.

_____. *This Most Famous Stream: The Liberal Democratic Way of Life.* Toronto, The Ryerson Press, 1954.

Manning, Helen Taft. *The Revolt of French Canada, 1800-1835: A Chapter in the History of the British Commonwealth.* Toronto, The Macmillan Company of Canada Limited, 1962.

Morris, Richard B. *The Emerging Nations and the American Revolution.* New York, Harper and Row, 1970.

Neufeld, E P ed. *Money and Banking in Canada: Historical Documents and Commentary.* Toronto, McClelland and Stewart Ltd, 1964.

Ouellet, Fernand. *Histoire Economique et Social du Quebec 1760-1850: Structures et Conjoncture,* Montreal, Fides, 1966.

Porter, Glenn and Robert Cuff, ed. *Enterprise and National Development: Essays in Canadian Business and Economic History.* Toronto, Hakkert, 1973.

Russell, Peter, ed. *Nationalism in Canada.* Toronto, McGraw-Hill Company of Canada Ltd, 1966.

Teeple, Gary, ed. *Capitalism and the National Question in Canada.* University of Toronto Press, 1972.

Wren, Melvin C. *The Course of Russian History.* New York, The Macmillan Company, 1968.